SANDY BONSIB

Sweet *treats*

12 DELECTABLE QUILTS FROM 2 EASY BLOCKS

10 Delicious Dessert Recipes

C&T PUBLISHING

Text and Artwork © 2007 Sandy Bonsib

Artwork © 2007 C&T Publishing, Inc.

Publisher: Amy Marson

Editorial Director: Gailen Runge

Acquisitions Editor: Jan Grigsby

Editor: Lynn Koolish

Technical Editors: Ellen Pahl and Elin Thomas

Copyeditor: Stacy Chamness

Proofreader: Wordfirm Inc.

Design Director/Cover & Book Designer: Christina D. Jarumay

Illustrators: Kim Jackson and Richard Sheppard

Production Coordinator: Matt Allen

Photography by C&T Publishing, Inc., unless otherwise noted

Published by C&T Publishing, Inc., P.O. Box 1456, Lafayette, CA 94549

Library of Congress Cataloging-in-Publication Data

Bonsib, Sandy.

  Sweet treats : 12 delectable quilts from 2 easy blocks / Sandy Bonsib.

    p. cm.

  ISBN-13: 978-1-57120-423-3 (paper trade : alk. paper)

  ISBN-10: 1-57120-423-7 (paper trade : alk. paper)

  1. Patchwork–Patterns. 2. Quilting–Patterns. 3. Desserts. I. Title.

  TT835.B62825 2007

  746.46'041–dc22

                    2007003436

Printed in China

10 9 8 7 6 5 4 3 2 1

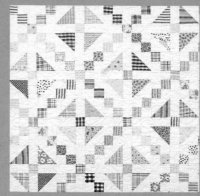

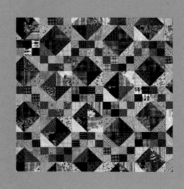

Contents

Acknowledgments

My first thank-you in all of my books is to my husband, John Bickley. After 26 years of marriage, he is still the nicest guy in the world. He is amazingly supportive in so many ways, and I wouldn't have the time and energy to create books without his tireless help.

Thank you to my wonderful, loyal students. Some of you have taken all of the Sweet Treats workshops just to play with Half-Square triangles and Four-Patches, and eat sweet treats! You have given me suggestions for quilt ideas and colors. You have laughed through the classes when we joked that this was really group therapy, not quilting. You have come to class after class, and I consider you my dear friends. Thank you from the bottom of my heart. I couldn't have done this book without you either.

Thank you to Becky Kraus, who does a wonderful job quilting my quilts for me. Her creativity never ceases to amaze me.

Thank you to Lynn Koolish, my editor. It has been a pleasure to work with her. Her expertise, hard work, and positive attitude are wonderful.

And, finally, thank you to C&T Publishing for believing in me. It has been a pleasure to work with you all for the very first time.

Introduction

*T*he concept of combining quilts and desserts evolved innocently enough. In February 2004 my dear friend and mentor Trish Carey and I were discussing, over coffee and scones, what classes I could teach at In The Beginning Fabrics, the wonderful quilt shop in Seattle where I taught for 15 years. (I now teach at a wonderful quilt shop, Quiltworks Northwest, in Bellevue, Washington, since In The Beginning closed in April 2006.) Trish scheduled In The Beginning's classes. In the process of brainstorming, we began talking about how much fun it would be to coordinate food, especially desserts, with quilts. Trish and I both love desserts, so the idea of quilts and food was appealing. And funny. We laughed at what we thought was a silly idea. Little did we know where this idea would go!

Since starting the Quilter's Dessert Series in the summer of 2004 with the first quilts and the first classes, *Lemon Chiffon One* and *Lemon Chiffon, Too*, there have been many more quilts in the series and desserts to go with them. Why, you might wonder, were there **two** first quilts? That's another story. I've never made a quilt that I wouldn't change something about if I made it again, and *Lemon Chiffon One* was no exception.

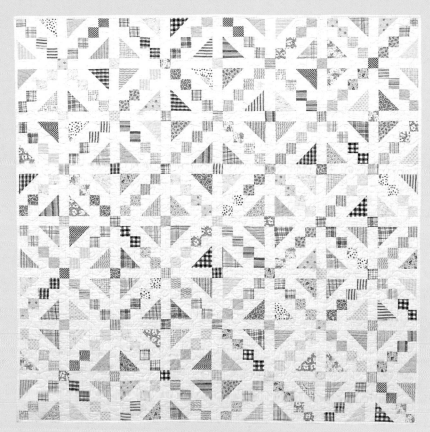

Lemon Chiffon One

The concept behind *Lemon Chiffon One* is working with all light values—light background fabric and light values of assorted colors.

Everything would be light, so the contrast would be subtle, I thought. I had no trouble choosing a light background fabric, and I didn't think I had trouble choosing light-value fabrics for the other colors. I chose all the lights of a single color, for example, light blues. In the light blue pile, I chose the very lightest blues. I did this for all the colors. I expected a quilt that had some contrast, but not much. To my surprise I discovered, when the quilt was finished, that the light colors look medium in value next to the almost-white background. So, although I love *Lemon Chiffon One* and it has been a very popular quilt, I decided to try again to get more blending but with some contrast. *Lemon Chiffon, Too* uses the same fabrics (yes, the exact same ones) as *Lemon Chiffon One*.

Lemon Chiffon, Too

I did, however, change the background fabric to a not-quite-so-light fabric. It's a creamy fabric with a blue design on it, so it doesn't read as light as the background fabric in *Lemon Chiffon One*.

Lemon Chiffon, Too did what I wanted *Lemon Chiffon One* to do, so I moved on, and I created a lemon chiffon pie recipe to go with my Lemon Chiffon Quilts!

Next, I decided to work with all medium values, creating *Caramel Sundae* (and homemade caramel sauce). The next quilt was *Chocolate Decadence*, working with all dark values, and creating a chocolate (my favorite food) dessert by the same name.

Making desserts was especially fun. My best friend's twin twenty-year-old sons were my taste testers (and I never found a dessert they wouldn't eat, no matter how it turned out). I started by looking in cookbooks and online

for desserts with the same names as my quilts. Then I started cooking. I never made a dessert exactly from the recipes I found. I always changed them by adding or deleting ingredients, taste testing, and trying again. I wanted my desserts to be unique, easy to prepare, and delicious. I hope you enjoy each and every one of them.

Working with the concept of value with quilts and desserts to match proved to be addictive. When I teach the classes locally I take the matching dessert for the students to eat. Everyone spends six hours sewing, chatting, and eating. It doesn't get much better than that!

And so I carried on, and over the next year and a half I created additional quilts and desserts of the same name: *Blueberry Cobbler*, working with all blues; *Mud Pie*, working with all three values—lights, mediums, and darks; *Mud Pie Leftovers*, working with the many Four-Patch blocks I didn't use in *Mud Pie* (and who doesn't like leftovers?); *Apple Crisp*, working with neutrals; *Pumpkin Pie*, working with a single color again—rust (dark burnt orange); *Hot Fudge Sundae*, working with black, white, and a touch of red; *Periwinkle Cupcake,* working with blue violet; and *Key Lime Pie*, working with two complementary colors, red violet and yellow green.

I never expected my first quilts and desserts to evolve into a book. As I write this, more desserts and quilts are in the making—and tasting—stages. Look for more quilts and desserts in the future!

Color and Value

When we see a quilt we like in a quilt show, on the wall of a quilt shop, or in a book, we often say, "Ooh, I love that quilt." We are usually referring to the colors in the quilt—the colors of the fabrics, the way these colors are used in the blocks, and their placement throughout the quilt. We don't usually say, "Ooh, I love that quilt. Look at the values. Look at how the lights, mediums, and darks are used."

Yes, we love color. We think quilts are great because of the colors. We look for fabrics to make a quilt we saw and loved—the **same** fabric, if possible, that the quilter used. Many of us are disappointed if we can't find that exact fabric. But it is not color that makes a quilt "work" and the design stand out; It's the **value** of those colors

WHAT IS VALUE?

The definition of value is the degree of lightness or darkness of a color. Value is related to color, but it is not the same thing. All of the rectangles below are blue. That is the color. But they aren't all the same; some are lighter and some are darker. That is the value.

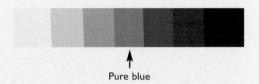

Pure blue

Blue color bars

The middle rectangle is considered the pure color. It's like the color that comes out of the box of eight crayons. When you add white to the pure color, you get the lighter values, in this case the lighter blues. The more white you add, the lighter the color. In the progression from the pure color to the left, the blue gets lighter and lighter.

When you add black, you get the darker values. The more black you add, the darker the color gets. In the progression from the pure color to the right, the blue gets darker and darker.

Here are more examples of value using purple, red, and red-violet. Again, the pure color is in the middle, the lighter values are on the left, and the darker values are on the right.

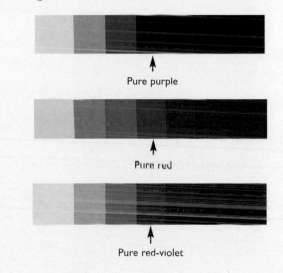

Pure purple

Pure red

Pure red-violet

Color bars in purple, red, red-violet

In general, we divide value into three categories: lights, mediums, and darks. The lights are on the left end of the color bar, the darks on the right end, and the mediums in the middle. Where does a color stop being light and become medium? Or stop being medium and become dark? There is no single answer to that question. The important concept is to see and identify the value of the fabric, not the color, so you put contrasting fabrics next to each other.

When you place a light next to a medium, a medium next to a dark, or a light next to a dark, you will have contrast. Light next to dark produces the highest contrast, but the other examples produce enough contrast for the design to work.

Light next to medium

Medium next to dark

Light next to dark

Usually, when you place two lights or two mediums or two darks next to each other, you will not have contrast, although there are exceptions.

Medium is a broad category. Some mediums are closer to the light end, but not really light. Some are closer to the dark end, but not really dark. To see if you have contrast with two mediums that you would like to use next to each other, step back and view them from a distance. You will immediately know whether they blend or contrast with each other.

Mediums that don't contrast

A star doesn't look like a star when the design blends with the background. In the examples at right, notice that the stars in both photographs are made up of the same units: five squares and four Half-Square triangles. Both blocks are made the same way, but in the block that uses contrasting values, you can see the star. In the block without contrasting values, you can't see the star. Most of us want to see a star if we take the time to make one. Blending is not what we want.

Star block with contrast

Star block that blends
(Look closely for the star points.)

It is the **contrast** between the fabrics that makes the design appear. If you can correctly identify the value of the fabrics you want to place next to each other, you will be able to get the contrast. This works with any fabrics in any colors because value provides the contrast; the color does not. Correctly identifying values is the key. And, unlike the color bars (page 7), most fabrics that we use are not solids. They are prints and often have multiple colors in them. How do you tell values then?

Step back. And I don't mean just three or four feet. Step back ten or fifteen or twenty feet. Go across the room or stand in the doorway. Use a vertical surface like a design wall so that everything is the same distance from your eye. Place your fabrics next to each other or overlapping to see if you can tell from a distance where one fabric ends and the other begins. Remember, they must be touching or overlapping. If you don't have a design wall, place your fabrics over the back of a sofa or chair, over the end of an ironing board, or have someone hold them for you. The key is making them vertical and getting far enough away from them to see if there is contrast. Another important reason to place your fabrics vertically and to step back is that you will then see the fabric as a whole. This process allows you to see the fabrics at a distance as you would see a finished quilt when it is on a wall or on a bed.

Take the time and make sure, from the very beginning of your project, that you have contrast before you make all your blocks. When you take the time to look, you will immediately see whether something reads light or not, or dark or not, or whether fabrics blend when they touch each other. Listen to those gut feelings. Don't rationalize because you love those two fabrics and really, really want to use them next to each other. If there isn't contrast, you aren't going to like the block, even if the fabrics are your two most favorite fabrics on earth.

VALUE IS RELATIVE

How do you translate this into choosing fabrics for your quilts? When you are choosing fabrics for a quilt, stack your bolts either vertically or horizontally, step back ten or more feet, and see if the lights **really** look light, if the mediums **really** look medium, and if the darks **really** look dark. If not, you don't **really** have those values. You're not sure? Ask a customer nearby or someone who works in a fabric store or the friend you brought with you—or all three. Quilters love to be helpful, and people in general love to give their opinions. Let them. If you don't agree, ignore them. After all, this is your quilt. But their information can help you, too. It is better to discover while you are choosing your fabric that you don't have lights or darks or both (mediums aren't usually a problem; most of us have plenty of those in our stash). It is worse to discover this after you have made twenty or forty blocks. Remember, the value of a fabric depends on the fabrics next to it.

Look at the Nine-Patch blocks below. Tan is the darkest fabric in the block on the left. It is the lightest in the block on the right.

In the next pair of Nine-Patch blocks, the rust fabric is the darkest in the one on the left, but the lightest in the one on the right. In general, rust is not dark, but when compared to something lighter, it is the darker of the two fabrics, and when compared to something darker, it is the lighter of the two. The rust didn't change; what is next to it did.

When you want to duplicate a quilt that you've seen, you can do this, even if the original quilt and your duplicate do not have a single piece of fabric in common! How? By duplicating the colors, the values of those colors, and the proportions of the colors and values in the original quilt. In other words, if a quilt is red and green, you will obviously use red and green fabrics. If it is dark green and medium red, use those values. Don't throw in some medium or light greens because you like them. And if there is only a touch of green, or a touch of black, or a touch of white, use only that much in your quilt, too. If you change the colors, the values, or the proportions, you will have a quilt that looks different than the original. If you don't, you won't. Your quilt will look almost identical to the original quilt from a distance (on a bed or on a wall) even if the two don't have a single piece of fabric in common.

TOOLS TO DETERMINE VALUE

DISTANCE

Distance—ten feet or more—is your best tool to determine value. Step back and squint at your fabrics when they are stacked vertically or horizontally. By squinting, you blur what you are seeing. (Some of us just need to remove our glasses to blur what we are seeing, and that's okay, too!) You filter out the details and see the fabric as a whole, which helps you determine, or read, the value. What you are trying to do is ignore the colors and look only at the values—the lightness or darkness of the colors. This is hard for us. We love color. How can we ignore it?

PHOTOCOPYING

Try photocopying. Cut small swatches of the fabrics you are planning to use in a quilt, and place the swatches on the glass of a black-and-white copier, and make a copy. You will see your fabrics in black and white and shades of gray. No color. You will have no trouble putting them in order from light to dark. You will have no trouble determining their value. Soon you'll be able to do this without a copier. Ignore the color. Try to see the lightness or darkness of a color only. This is hard, but you will get better with practice.

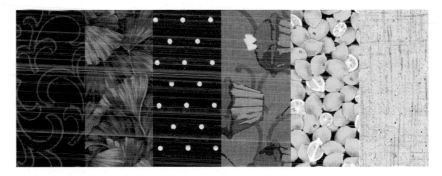

Fabric swatches

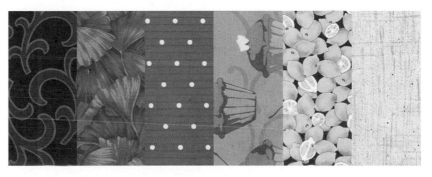

Photocopies of the fabric swatches

COLOR FILTERS

Color filters are pieces of red or green plastic used to evaluate the values of your fabrics. Red filters are for all fabrics that aren't in the red color family, and green filters are for all fabrics not in the green color family. The filters take away some but not all of the color, helping you to see the values better.

Red and green color filters, also known as value finders

REDUCING GLASS

A reducing glass is the opposite of a magnifying glass, and can be found in most quilt stores. By making things smaller, it helps you to read the value easier; it's like looking at something from a distance.

CAMERA

Look through a camera. It, too, makes things smaller so you can read the value.

PEEPHOLE

A peephole, like those used in doors to see who is outside, is not my favorite tool because it is often curved. I think the curvature distorts, but an advantage is that peepholes are small and fit easily in your purse or pocket.

We often have our favorite value, and it is hard to choose others. Most of us like mediums. Lights or darks are difficult to choose, but choose them anyway. Remember those piles of lights, mediums, and darks? Use them to tell you what you need when you go shopping. Although it may be hard to choose one value (for me, choosing lights is the hardest), force yourself. In general, your quilts will be more eye-catching, have greater depth, and be more interesting to look at if you use all three values in your work. Always remember: Color gets all the credit in a quilt, but value does all the work. If you have chosen the fabrics and like the colors, then you will like the blocks if you have contrast. If you don't, you won't like the blocks no matter how beautiful the colors are. We think a quilt is beautiful because of the colors in it, but it is the value contrast that makes those fabrics work together to create a beautiful quilt.

Easy Construction, Complex Look

I never would have guessed I could create so many different quilts using such simple units: Half-Square triangles and Four-Patch blocks. Look carefully at all the quilts in this book, and you will see that they are all made from Half-Square triangles, Four-Patches, and a few additional squares and rectangles. The cutting is easy because it is done from strips.

HALF-SQUARE TRIANGLE BLOCKS

Each project has the specific instructions needed to make the blocks. I make my Half-Square triangles a little oversize and trim them. Why? For accuracy and ease in sewing everything together. Half-Square triangles have a tendency to be a little too big or a little too small, or have concave edges or convex edges. It is difficult to create an accurate square. We all take a slightly different seam allowance. We all press a little differently. Some fabrics have more stretch than others. To compensate for these factors, you will make the Half-Square triangles slightly larger than they need to be, then trim them down to the exact size. Rather than adding ⅞" to the desired finished size triangle, I add 1".

1. Layer 2 squares. Mark the diagonal line on the back of the lighter square of the pair.

Draw diagonal line.

2. Sew the layered squares together a scant ¼"* away from the diagonal line on both sides, and cut on the diagonal line to make 2 Half-Square triangles. Press the seam allowance to one side, usually toward the darker fabric.

*Note: A scant ¼" seam is slightly less than a full measured ¼" seam, but is not so small that it is an ⅛" seam.

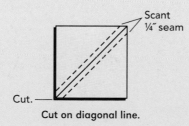

Cut on diagonal line.

3. To trim the pieced squares, line up the 45° line on a 6" bias square ruler or other 6" square ruler with the diagonal seam. Trim the top and side just enough to square up the corner.

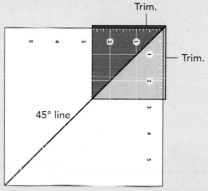

Line up with 45° line and trim.

4. Remove the ruler, and rotate the pieced unit 180°. Again, line up the 45° line of the ruler with the diagonal seam. Align the trimmed sides with the desired size on the ruler. Trim the remaining sides.

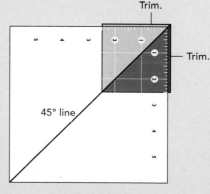

Align and trim.

Projects

The projects in this book are designed so that you can do one of the following:

- Use many fabrics from your stash, giving the quilts a scrappy look
- Use fewer fabrics and purchase yardage
- Use a combination of scraps and yardage

The project instructions include the amount of fabric to buy if you are purchasing, or you can refer to the cutting instructions to see exactly how big each piece of fabric needs to be so you can use fabrics from your stash.

Note that the yardage requirements are generous to allow for shrinkage and a cutting mistake or two. If you don't have enough scraps to make a particular quilt, buying fabric will certainly help you build a stash of fabric scraps to make more quilts!

With each quilt, you'll be able to practice using color and value effectively. Before you start a project, take a look at the quilts at the end of the project instructions to see how some of my students chose to interpret the project quilt with their own colors and values.

WORKING WITH LIGHT VALUES AND MANY COLORS

Lemon Chiffon One Quilt

Lemon Chiffon, Too Quilt

WORKING WITH DARK VALUES AND TWO COLORS

Chocolate Decadence Quilt

WORKING WITH MEDIUM VALUES AND MANY COLORS

Caramel Sundae Quilt

WORKING WITH THREE VALUES AND MANY COLORS

Mud Pie Quilt

Mud Pie Leftovers Quilt

WORKING WITH THREE VALUES AND NEUTRALS

Apple Crisp Quilt

WORKING WITH MEDIUM AND DARK VALUES AND ONE COLOR

Blueberry Cobbler Quilt

WORKING WITH THREE VALUES AND ONE COLOR

Pumpkin Pie Quilt

Periwinkle Cupcake Quilt

WORKING WITH THREE VALUES, NEUTRALS, AND AN ACCENT COLOR

Hot Fudge Sundae Quilt with a Cherry on Top

WORKING WITH THREE VALUES AND TWO COMPLEMENTARY COLORS

Key Lime Pie Quilt

Lemon Chiffon
One Quilt

*T*his quilt includes many colors but mainly one value—lights. In this quilt you will work with light values and white to create subtle contrast. Notice that I used the word *subtle*. The contrast will not be high. In this quilt, I used different colored fabrics and a single background fabric. For the colored fabrics, I chose small prints, plaids, and stripes. When you choose your fabrics, make sure they are mainly light values. Be careful not to choose very many medium values. Because the background is almost white, any medium values will look dark by comparison.

FINISHED QUILT SIZE
59″ × 59″

note:

This is a scrappy quilt. If you plan to work from your stash, refer to Cutting (below) for the specific sizes of each fabric. If you plan to buy fabric, refer to Yardage for what you need to purchase.

YARDAGE

- 32 different fabrics for blocks:

  - ¼ yard each of 4 different yellow fabrics

  - ¼ yard each of 4 different light blue fabrics

  - ¼ yard each of 4 different light red fabrics

  - ¼ yard each of 4 different light purple fabrics

  - ¼ yard each of 4 different light pink fabrics

  - ¼ yard each of 4 different light black-and-white prints

  - ¼ yard each of 4 different light green fabrics

  - ¼ yard each of 4 different light gold or tan prints

- Light background and binding fabric: 3½ yards

- Backing Fabric: 3⅝ yards

- Batting: 64″ x 64″

CUTTING

Colored fabrics for blocks

- From each of the 32 different fabrics, cut 1 strip 4″ × 42″.

  From each strip cut 2 squares 4″ × 4″ for a total of 64 squares for Half-Square triangle blocks and 1 strip 2″ × 20″ for a total of 32 strips for Four-Patch blocks.

- From the remaining colored fabrics, cut 49 squares 2″ × 2″ for sashing squares. Use a variety of the colors.

Background fabric

- Cut 64 squares 4″ × 4″ for Half-Square triangle blocks.

- Cut 32 strips 2″ × 20″ for Four-Patch blocks.

- Cut 112 rectangles 2″ × 6½″ for sashing.

- Cut 7 strips 2″ × 42″ for binding.

CONSTRUCTION

Make sure your ¼″ seam allowance is accurate—all blocks assume an accurate ¼″ seam.

HALF-SQUARE TRIANGLES

Use 64 of the 4″ × 4″ colored squares and the 64 of the 4″ × 4″ background squares, to make 128 Half-Square triangle blocks. Each pair of squares yields 2 Half-Square triangle blocks.

1. Pair 1 colored and 1 background square right sides together. Draw a diagonal line on the wrong side of the lighter square. Note: This will be the cutting line, not the sewing line.

Draw diagonal line.

2. Draw another set of lines a scant ¼″ from the drawn lines. These are your sewing lines. If you have a ¼″ presser foot, you can omit this step. Sew a scant ¼″ away from the center line on both sides.

Sew scant ¼″ from center line.

3. Cut on the center line.

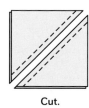

Cut.

4. Press the seam allowances toward the darker fabric.

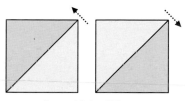

Press. Make 128.

5. Trim each block to 3½″ × 3½″. (See page 13 for trimming instructions.)

FOUR-PATCH UNITS

Use 32 of the 2″ wide colored strips and 32 of the 2″-wide background strips to make Four-Patch blocks.

1. Pair 1 colored strip and 1 background strip right sides together. Sew the strips together.

Sew strips together.

2. Press the seam toward the darker fabric. Cut the strips into 8 segments, each 2″ wide.

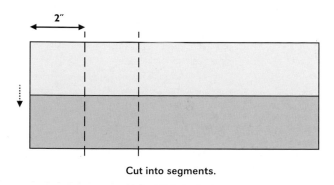

2″

Cut into segments.

3. Arrange 2 segments as shown, and sew them together.

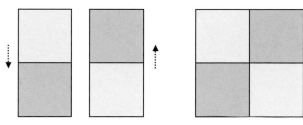

Sew into Four-Patch blocks. Make 128.

ASSEMBLING THE BLOCKS

1. Arrange 2 Half-Square triangle blocks and 2 Four-Patch blocks as shown. Note the placement of the background fabric.

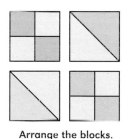

Arrange the blocks.

2. Sew the blocks together to make a Lemon Chiffon block. Press the seams as indicated.

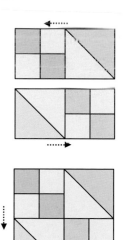

Make 64.

ASSEMBLING THE QUILT TOP

Refer to the Quilt Assembly Diagram.

1. Arrange the blocks, sashing rectangles, and 2″ × 2″ colored squares. Sew them together into rows. Press the seams toward the sashing strips.

2. Sew the rows together. Press the seams toward the sashing rows.

3. Layer the top with the batting and backing. Quilt and bind as desired (see page 86).

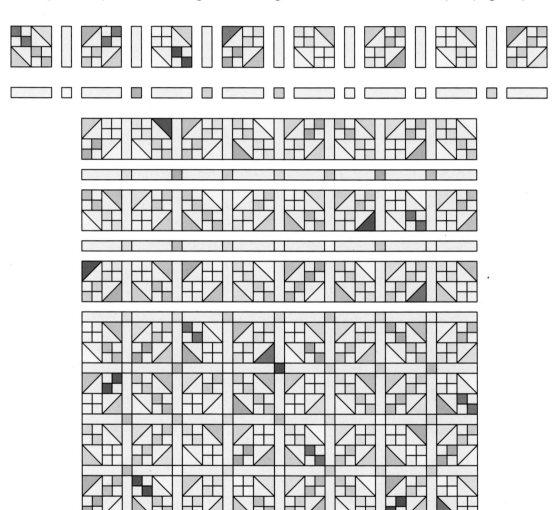

Quilt Assembly Diagram

Lemon Chiffon, Too Quilt

As with *Lemon Chiffon One*, this quilt includes many colors in only light values. In this quilt, I used the same fabrics as I did in *Lemon Chiffon One*. I also used a single background fabric, but for this quilt, the background fabric, although light in value, wasn't nearly as light as the background fabric in *Lemon Chiffon One*. Therefore, the contrast between the background fabric and the rest of the colored fabrics is more subtle. This is the effect I wanted in *Lemon Chiffon One*. It took me a second try to get it!

FINISHED QUILT SIZE
44¼″ × 55″

note:

This is a scrappy quilt. If you plan to work from your stash, refer to Cutting (below) for the specific sizes of each fabric. If you plan to buy fabric, refer to Yardage for what you need to purchase.

YARDAGE

- 32 different fabrics for blocks:

  - ⅛ yard each of 4 different yellow fabrics

  - ⅛ yard each of 4 different light blue fabrics

  - ⅛ yard each of 4 different light red fabrics

  - ⅛ yard each of 4 different light purple fabrics

  - ⅛ yard each of 4 different light pink fabrics

  - ⅛ yard each of 4 different light black-and-white prints

  - ⅛ yard each of 4 different light green fabrics

  - ⅛ yard each of 4 different light gold or tan prints

- Background and binding fabric: 3 yards

- Backing fabric: 3 yards

- Batting: 50″ × 60″

CUTTING

Colored fabrics for blocks

- From each of the 32 different fabrics, cut 2 squares 4″ × 4″ for a total of 64 squares for Half-Square triangle blocks.

- From the remaining colored fabrics, cut 32 squares 2″ × 2″ for block centers. Use a variety of colors.

Background fabric

- Cut 64 squares 4″ × 4″ for Half-Square triangle blocks.

- Cut 128 rectangles 2″ × 3½″ for blocks.

- Cut 4 squares 13½″ × 13½″. Cut the squares diagonally twice to make 16 side triangles (you will need only 14).

- Cut 2 squares 8″ × 8″. Cut the squares diagonally once to make 4 corner triangles.

- Cut 6 strips 2″ × 42″ for binding.

CONSTRUCTION

Make sure your ¼″ seam allowance is accurate—all blocks assume an accurate ¼″ seam.

HALF-SQUARE TRIANGLES

Use 64 of the 4″ × 4″ colored squares and 64 of the 4″ × 4″ background squares to make 128 Half-Square triangle blocks. Each pair of squares yields 2 Half-Square triangle blocks.

1. Pair 1 colored and 1 background square right sides together. Draw a diagonal line on the wrong side of the lighter square. Note: This will be the cutting line, not the sewing line.

Draw diagonal line.

2. Draw another set of lines a scant ¼″ from the drawn lines. These are your sewing lines. If you have a ¼″ presser foot, you can omit this step. Sew a scant ¼″ away from the center line on both sides.

Sew scant ¼″ from center line.

3. Cut on the center line.

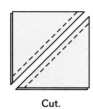

Cut.

4. Press the seam allowances toward the darker fabric.

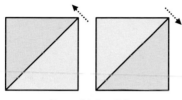

Press. Make 128.

5. Trim each block to 3½″ × 3½″. (See page 13 for trimming instructions.)

ASSEMBLING THE BLOCKS

1. Arrange 4 Half-Square triangle blocks, 4 rectangles 2″ × 3½″, and 1 colored 2″ × 2″ square. Note the placement of the background fabric.

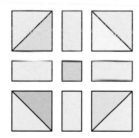

Arrange blocks, rectangles, and squares.

2. Sew the blocks together to make a Lemon Chiffon block. Press the seams as indicated.

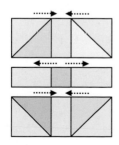

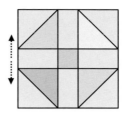

Press. Make 32.

ASSEMBLING THE QUILT TOP

Refer to the Quilt Assembly Diagram on page 22.

1. Arrange the blocks and side triangles as shown.

2. Sew the blocks and side triangles together in diagonal rows.

3. Press the seams in opposite directions from row to row.

4. Add the corner triangles last. Press the seams toward the corner triangles.

5. Trim the edges 1″ from the points of the blocks.

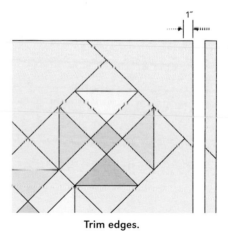

Trim edges.

6. Layer the top with the batting and backing. Quilt and bind as desired (see page 86).

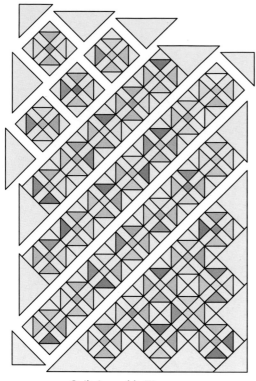

Quilt Assembly Diagram

Strawberry Lime Chiffon Pie,
Cate Franklin,
62¼″ x 71¼″
(Quilted by Becky Kraus)

Lemon Chiffon Pie
with Graham Cracker Crust

INGREDIENTS

- 1 envelope unflavored gelatin
- ¾ cup sugar
- 4 eggs, separated
- ½ cup water
- ½ cup lemon juice
- 1 teaspoon finely shredded lemon zest
- ½ cup whipping cream

Crust
- ⅓ cup butter or margarine
- ¼ cup sugar
- 1¼ cups finely crushed graham crackers (about 18 crackers)

1. To prepare the crust, melt the butter or margarine. Stir in the sugar. Add crushed graham crackers and mix well. Spread the mixture evenly into a 9-inch pie plate. Press onto the bottom and sides to form a firm, even crust. Chill about 1 hour or until firm.

2. In a saucepan combine unflavored gelatin and ½ cup sugar.

3. Beat together slightly beaten egg yolks, water, and lemon juice. Stir into the gelatin mixture. Cook and stir until the mixture boils and the gelatin dissolves.

4 Remove from the heat. Stir in lemon zest.

5. Place in refrigerator and chill to the consistency of corn syrup, stirring occasionally. Remove from the refrigerator (the mixture will continue to set).

6. Immediately beat egg whites until soft peaks form. Gradually add ¼ cup sugar, beating until stiff peaks form.

7. When the gelatin is partially set (to the consistency of unbeaten egg whites), fold in the stiff-beaten whites.

8. Beat whipping cream until soft peaks form. Fold into the gelatin mixture. Chill until the mixture mounds when spooned. Spoon into the graham cracker crust. Chill for 4 hours or until firm.

Chocolate Decadence Quilt

*T*his two-color quilt features primarily one value, darks. I chose dark red and black, but you can choose any two dark colors. My students did just that with color combinations of all sorts! Make sure that the majority of colors you choose really are dark, not medium or medium dark. An occasional medium, however, adds a bright spot to the quilt, making it more interesting. Notice that some black fabrics don't read dark if they have light designs on them. Choose carefully. For this quilt, the contrast is very subtle; I had to finish all of the blocks and arrange them before I really noticed it. In the process of creating the blocks, I wondered whether I would have enough contrast when the quilt was finished. I found I did indeed.

FINISHED QUILT SIZE

58″ × 65¼″

note:

This is a scrappy quilt. If you plan to work from your stash, refer to Cutting (below) for the specific sizes of each fabric. If you plan to buy fabric, refer to Yardage for what you need to purchase.

YARDAGE

- ¼ yard each of 18 different dark red prints for blocks
- ⅓ yard each of 18 different black prints for blocks
- Backing fabric: 3⅝ yards (horizontal seam)
- Binding fabric: ⅜ yard
- Batting: 64″ × 72″

CUTTING

Dark red fabrics

- From each of the 18 dark red fabrics, cut 1 strip 6″ × 22″.

  From each strip, cut 2 squares 6″ × 6″ for a total of 36 squares for Half-Square triangle blocks and cut 2 rectangles 3″ × 10″ for a total of 36 rectangles for Four-Patch blocks.

- From 1 red fabric, cut 2 more rectangles 3″ × 10″ for Four-Patch blocks.

Black fabrics

- From each of the 18 black fabrics, cut 1 strip 6″ × 22″.

  From each strip, cut 2 squares 6″ × 6″ for a total of 36 squares for Half-Square triangle blocks and cut 2 rectangles 3″ × 10″ for a total of 36 rectangles for Four-Patch blocks.

- From 1 black fabric, cut 2 more rectangles 3″ × 10″ for Four-Patch blocks.

- Cut 8 squares 9½″ × 9½″. Cut the squares diagonally twice to make 32 side triangles (2 are extra).

- Cut 2 squares 5½″ × 5½″. Cut the squares diagonally once to make 4 corner triangles.

Binding fabric

- Cut 7 strips 2″ × 42″.

CONSTRUCTION

Make sure your ¼″ seam allowance is accurate—all blocks assume an accurate ¼″ seam.

✳ *Although the directions specify dark red and black fabrics, if you chose different dark colors, substitute the colors you chose in the directions.*

HALF-SQUARE TRIANGLES

Use 36 of the 6″ × 6″ dark red squares and 36 of the 6″ × 6″ dark black squares to make 72 Half-Square triangle blocks. Each pair of squares yields 2 Half-Square triangle blocks

1. Pair 1 red and 1 black square right sides together. Draw a diagonal line on the wrong side of the lighter square. Note: This will be the cutting line, not the sewing line.

Draw diagonal line.

2. Draw another set of lines a scant ¼″ from the drawn lines. These are your sewing lines. If you have a ¼″ presser foot, you can omit this step. Sew a scant ¼″ away from the center line on both sides.

Sew scant ¼″ from center line.

3. Cut on the center line.

Cut.

4. Press the seam allowances toward the darker fabric.

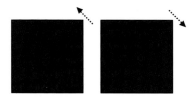

Press. Make 72.

5. Trim each block to 5½″ × 5½″. (See page 13 for trimming instructions.)

FOUR-PATCH BLOCKS

Use 38 of the 3″-wide red strips and 38 of the 3″-wide black strips to make Four-Patch bocks.

1. Pair 1 red strip and 1 black strip right sides together. Sew the strips together. Combine red and black strips together in matching pairs.

Sew strips together.

2. Press the seam toward the darker fabric. Cut the strips into 3 segments, each 3″ wide, for a total of 6 matching pairs.

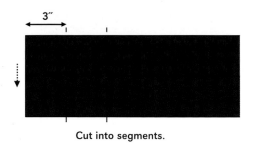

Cut into segments.

3. Arrange 2 segments as shown, and sew them together. Make 3 identical blocks from each matching pair of strip sets.

Sew into Four-Patch blocks. Make 56.

ASSEMBLING THE QUILT TOP

Refer to the Quilt Assembly Diagram on page 27.

1. Arrange the Half-Square triangle blocks, Four-Patch blocks, and side triangles. Note the placement of the Half-Square triangle blocks on the outside edges of the quilt top. These Half-Square triangle blocks are turned so the red is nearest the outside edges.

2. Sew the blocks and side triangles together in diagonal rows. Press the seams in opposite directions from row to row.

3. Add the corner triangles last. Press the seams toward the corner triangles.

4. Trim the edges ¾″ from the points of the blocks.

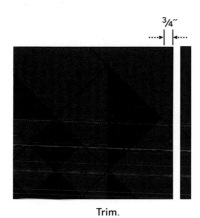

Trim.

5. Layer the top with the batting and backing. Quilt and bind as desired (see page 86).

Quilt Assembly Diagram

Life Is Like a Box of Chocolates,
Merry Maricich,
48½″ × 63¼″
(Quilted by Patsi Hanseth)

Chocolate! Chocolate Decadence,
Cate Franklin,
84″ × 89½″
(Quilted by Becky Kraus)

Triple Chocolate Decadence,
Joan E. Christ,
49½″ × 55¾″
(Quilted by Therese Strothman)

Chocolate Decadence Cupcakes

INGREDIENTS

Cupcakes

- 2 cups semisweet chocolate chips
- 6 ounces unsweetened chocolate
- ¾ cup butter
- ⅔ cup flour
- ½ teaspoon baking powder
- ½ teaspoon salt
- 6 eggs
- 2 cups sugar
- 4 teaspoons real vanilla extract
- Paper muffin cups (regular size)
- Cupcake pan (regular size, not mini)

Topping

- 1 cup heavy whipping cream
- 1 tablespoon sugar
- 1 teaspoon vanilla

1. Preheat oven to 350°.

2. Melt semisweet chips, unsweetened chocolate, and butter in microwave or in saucepan over low heat, stirring until smooth.

3. Stir flour, baking powder, and salt together.

4. In a large mixing bowl, beat eggs, sugar, and vanilla until fluffy. Beat in chocolate mixture. Add flour mixture. Chill until batter mounds with a spoon.

5. Drop by mounded tablespoons into paper muffin cups in cupcake pan, filling each cup ½ to ¾ full

6. Bake for 22 minutes. Test with a toothpick for doneness. Adjust cooking time as needed until toothpick comes out clean, but do not overbake.

Makes 22–24 cupcakes.

DECADENT TOPPING

Whip heavy whipping cream until it mounds slightly. Add sugar and vanilla. Finish whipping until peaks hold their shape. Put a generous dollop on top of each Chocolate Decadence Cupcake. If desired, garnish with chocolate shavings.

Caramel Sundae Quilt

_T_his quilt includes many colors but only one value—mediums. Notice that medium is a large category that includes mediums that are closer to lights, mediums that are closer to darks, and mediums that are really medium. The contrast in this quilt isn't as subtle as that in the previous quilts because you are using color differences to create the contrast, even though you are again working with a single value. A medium-value gold was used in each of the blocks along with another contrasting color. Don't worry about matching fabrics. This is a scrap quilt. Variety makes it work and keeps it interesting. Having said that, you don't need to make it as scrappy as I have. Feel free to choose fewer fabrics and repeat them. I suggest avoiding large-scale prints that might not read medium when cut into small pieces. However, one of my students, Mary Washer, ignored my advice completely and made a beautiful Caramel Sundae quilt with green medium- and large-scale fabrics! (See page 33.)

FINISHED QUILT SIZE
80½″ × 80½″

note:

This is a scrappy quilt. If you plan to work from your stash, refer to Cutting (below) for the specific sizes of each fabric. If you plan to buy fabric, refer to Yardage for what you need to purchase.

YARDAGE

- ¼ yard each of 26 different medium-value fabrics for blocks

- ¼ yard each of 26 different fabrics in one color family for background (gold is the background color family in the pictured quilt)

- Backing fabric: 5 yards*

- Binding fabric: ⅔ yard

- Batting: 86″ × 86″

*If your backing fabric is less than 44″ wide, you will need 7¼ yards.

CUTTING

Medium value fabrics

- From each of the 26 fabrics, cut 1 strip 5″ × 42″ for a total of 26 strips. (If you are using fat quarters, cut 2 strips 5″ × 22″ from each for a total of 52 strips.)

From each 5″ × 42″ strip (or from 1 strip that is 5″ × 22″), cut 4 squares 5″ × 5″ for a total of 104 squares for Half-Square triangle blocks.

From each remaining 5″ × 22″ strip, cut 2 strips 2½″ × 22″ for a total of 52 strips for Four-Patch blocks.

Medium-value background fabrics

- From each of the 26 fabrics, cut 1 strip 5″ × 42″ for a total of 26 strips. (If you are using fat quarters, cut 2 strips 5″ × 22″ for a total of 52 strips.)

From each 5″ × 42″ strip (or from 1 strip that is 5″ × 22″), cut 4 squares 5″ × 5″ for a total of 104 squares for Half-Square triangle blocks.

From each remaining 5″ × 22″ strip, cut 2 strips 2½″ × 22″ for a total of 52 strips for Four-Patch blocks.

Binding fabric

- Cut 9 strips 2″ × 42″.

CONSTRUCTION

Make sure your ¼″ seam allowance is accurate—all blocks assume an accurate ¼″ seam.

HALF-SQUARE TRIANGLES

Use 104 of the 5″ × 5″ assorted colored squares and 104 of the 5″ × 5″ background squares to make 208 Half-Square triangle blocks. Each pair of squares yields 2 Half-Square triangle blocks.

1. Pair 1 assorted colored and 1 background square right sides together. Draw a diagonal line on the wrong side of the lighter square. Note: This will be the cutting line, not the sewing line.

Draw diagonal line.

2. Draw another set of lines a scant ¼″ from the drawn line. These are your sewing lines. If you have a ¼″ presser foot, you can omit this step. Sew a scant ¼″ away from the center line on both sides.

Sew scant ¼″ from center line.

3. Cut on the center line.

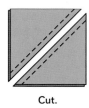

Cut.

4. Press the seam allowances toward the darker fabric.

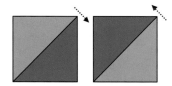

Press. Make 208.

5. Trim each block to 4½″ × 4½″. (See page 13 for trimming instructions.)

FOUR-PATCH BLOCKS

Use 52 of the 2½″-wide assorted color strips and 52 of the 2½″-wide background strips to make Four-Patch blocks.

1. Pair 1 assorted color strip and 1 background strip right sides together. Sew the strips together.

Sew strips together.

2. Press the seam toward the darker fabric. Cut the strips into 8 segments, each 2½″ wide.

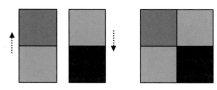

Cut into segments.

3. Arrange 2 segments randomly as shown, and sew them together.

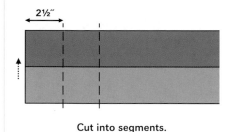

Sew into Four-Patch blocks. Make 208.

ASSEMBLING THE QUILT TOP

Refer to the Quilt Assembly Diagram.

1. Choose 192 Four-Patch blocks (you will have 16 left over). Arrange them with the 208 Half-Square triangle blocks. The setting is a Barn Raising with alternating Half-Square triangle and Four-Patch rows. Notice the small diamonds created by the Half-Square triangle blocks near the corners of the quilt.

2. Sew the blocks together in rows. Press the seams in opposite directions from row to row.

3. Sew the rows together. Press.

4. Layer the top with the batting and backing. Quilt and bind as desired (see page 86).

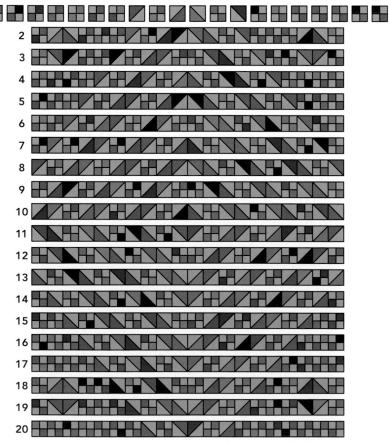

Quilt Assembly Diagram

Summer Punch,
Mary Louise Washer,
94½″ × 94¼″
(Quilted by Barbara Day)

Latté Lite,
Penny A. Hazelton,
94½″ × 94½″
(Quilted by Sue Lohse)

Homemade Caramel Sauce

INGREDIENTS

- 1½ cups light brown sugar, packed
- ½ cup light corn syrup
- ¼ cup butter
- ½ cup heavy whipping cream
- 1 teaspoon vanilla

1. Heat brown sugar, corn syrup, and butter over low heat to boiling, stirring constantly.

2. Remove from heat; stir in whipping cream and vanilla. Pour over ice cream. Store any extra in refrigerator.

3. Garnish with pecans or walnuts and whipped cream, if desired.

Mud Pie Quilt

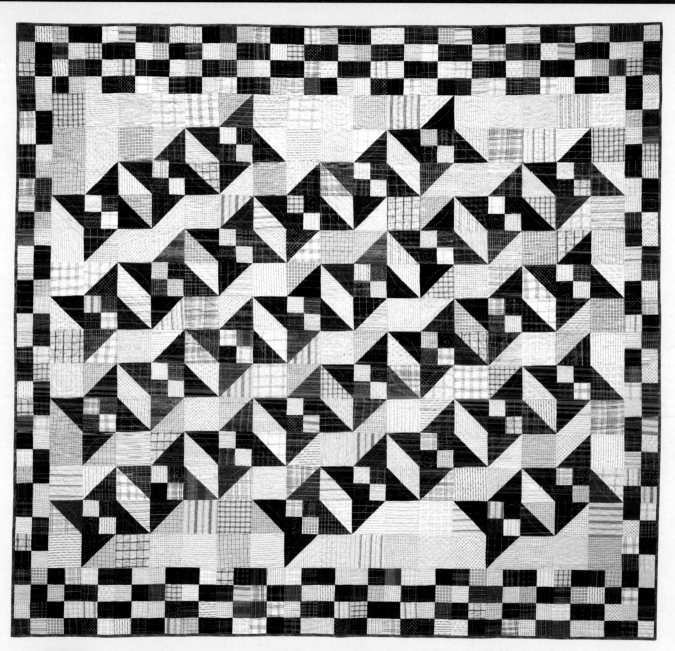

his multicolored quilt features all three values—lights, mediums, and darks. I used many colors, but you can choose just two or three colors if you like. You can also select a different fabric style. My quilt is all stripes and plaids, but yours could be all prints or a combination of prints and plaids, or all batiks. It's the values that are most important. Because you are working with all three values, your contrast will be obvious. Using all three values adds lots of depth and interest to your work. For the light values in this quilt, you can use neutrals such as white, cream, and/or tan, or you can use light values of one of the colors you are using, for example, light blues, light greens, and so on.

FINISHED QUILT SIZE

76½″ × 72½″

note:

Everyone loves leftovers, and you'll have 32 extra Half-Square triangle blocks, 24 extra Four-Patch blocks, and you can make many additional Four-Patch blocks from the extra strip sections. Make Mud Pie Leftovers (starting on page 39), or create your own new design. Have fun.

This is a scrappy quilt. If you plan to work from your stash, refer to Cutting (below) for the specific sizes of each fabric. If you plan to buy fabric, refer to Yardage for what you need to purchase.

YARDAGE

- ¼ yard each of 40 different medium- and dark-value fabrics for blocks and border

- ¼ yard each of 40 different light-value fabrics for background

- Backing fabric: 5 yards

- Binding fabric: ⅝ yard

- Batting: 82″ × 78″

CUTTING

Medium and dark fabrics

- From each of the 40 fabrics, cut 1 strip 5″ × 42″.

   From each strip, cut 2 squares 5″ × 5″ for a total of 80 squares for Half-Square triangle blocks.

   Cut the remainder of each strip in half, creating 2 strips 2½″ × 32″ for a total of 80 strips for Four-Patch blocks.

Light fabrics

- From each of the 40 fabrics, cut 1 strip 5″ × 42″.

   From each strip, cut 2 squares 5″ × 5″ for a total of 80 squares for Half-Square triangle blocks, and cut 2 squares 4½″ × 4½″ for a total of 80 squares for background.

   Cut the remainder of each strip in half, creating 2 strips 2½″ × 23″ for a total of 80 strips for Four-Patch blocks.

Binding fabric

- Cut 8 strips 2″ × 42″.

CONSTRUCTION

Make sure your ¼″ seam allowance is accurate—all blocks assume an accurate ¼″ seam.

HALF-SQUARE TRIANGLES

Use 80 medium and dark 5″ × 5″ squares and 80 light 5″ × 5″ squares to make 160 Half-Square triangle blocks. Each pair of squares yields 2 Half-Square triangle blocks.

1. Pair 1 medium or dark value square and 1 light square right sides together. Draw a diagonal line on the wrong side of the lighter square. Note: This will be the cutting line, not the sewing line.

Draw diagonal line.

2. Draw another set of lines a scant ¼″ from the drawn lines. These are your sewing lines. If you have a ¼″ presser foot, you can omit this step. Sew a scant ¼″ away from the center line on both sides.

Sew scant ¼″ from center line.

3. Cut on the center line.

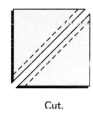

Cut.

4. Press the seam allowances toward the darker fabric.

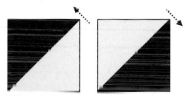

Press. Make 160.

5. Trim each block to 4½″ × 4½″. (See page 13 for trimming instructions.)

FOUR-PATCH BLOCKS

Use 40 of the 2½″-wide medium and dark strips, and 40 of the 2½″-wide light-value strips to make Four-Patch blocks. (The light strips will be shorter than the medium- and dark-value strips. This is okay.)

1. Pair 1 medium- or dark-value strip and 1 light strip right sides together. Sew the strips together.

Sew strips together.

2. Press the seam toward the darker fabric. Cut the strips into 8 segments, each 2½″ wide.

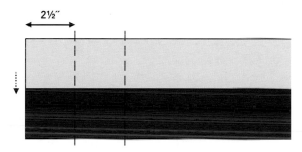

Cut into segments.

3. Arrange 2 segments randomly as shown, and sew them together.

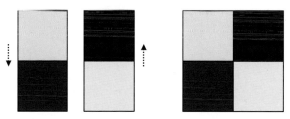

Sew into Four-Patch blocks. Make 160.

ASSEMBLING THE QUILT TOP

Refer to the Quilt Assembly Diagram.

1. Choose and arrange 128 Half-Square triangle blocks, 78 light 4½″ × 4½″ squares, and 136 Four-Patch blocks in 18 rows as shown. Note that 32 of the Four-Patch blocks are in the middle of the stars and 104 Four-Patch blocks create the borders.

2. Sew the entire quilt, both the star and border blocks, together in rows. Press the seams in opposite directions from row to row.

3. Sew the rows together. Press.

4. Layer the top with the batting and backing. Quilt and bind as desired (see page 86).

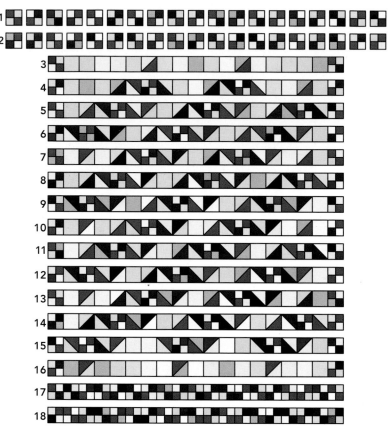

Quilt Assembly Diagram

Ballard Mud Pie, Joan E. Christ, 102″ × 74″ (Quilted by Therese Strothman)

SWEET TREATS

Mud Pie
Leftovers Quilt

*W*ho doesn't like leftovers once in awhile? When I finished *Mud Pie* (page 35), I had lots of Four-Patch blocks left. I also had many strips left so I could make even more Four-Patch blocks. I noticed that I didn't use as many Four-Patch blocks as I expected to use in *Mud Pie* because each star only features one Four-Patch, but there are four Half-Square triangles in each star. I created even more Four-Patches from the leftover strips, then placed them on point to create this smaller quilt of leftovers.

FINISHED QUILT SIZE
53″ × 58½″

note:

This is a scrappy quilt. If you plan to work from your stash, refer to Cutting (below). If you plan to buy fabric, refer to Yardage for what you need to purchase.

YARDAGE

- 1 fat eighth each of 21 different medium and dark plaids and stripes for Four-Patch blocks

- 1 fat eighth each of 21 different very light plaids and stripes for Four-Patch blocks

- 1 yard very light plaid or stripe for side and corner triangles

- Backing fabric: 3½ yards (horizontal seam)

- Binding fabric: ⅝ yard

- Batting: 59″ × 65″

CUTTING

Medium and dark plaids and stripes

- From each of the 21 different fabrics, cut 2 strips 2½″ × 21″ for a total of 42 strips for Four-Patch blocks.

Very light plaids and stripes

- From each of the 21 different fabrics, cut 2 strips 2½″ × 21″ for a total of 42 strips for Four-Patch blocks.

Very light plaid or stripe

- Cut 3 strips 8″ × 42″; from these strips cut 9 squares 9″ × 9″. Cut the squares diagonally twice to make 36 side triangles (you will need 34).

- Cut 2 squares 6″ × 6″. Cut these diagonally once to make 4 corner triangles.

CONSTRUCTION

Make sure your ¼″ seam allowance is accurate—all blocks assume an accurate ¼″ seam.

FOUR-PATCH BLOCKS

Use 42 of the 2½″-wide medium and dark plaid and stripe strips and 42 of the 2½″-wide very light plaid and stripe strips to make 162 Four-Patch blocks.

1. Pair 1 medium or dark plaid or stripe strip and 1 very light plaid or stripe strip right sides together. Sew the strips together.

Sew strips together.

2. Press the seams toward the medium or dark fabric. Cut the strips into 8 segments, each 2½″ wide.

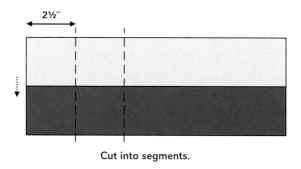

Cut into segments.

3. Arrange 2 segments randomly as shown, and sew them together.

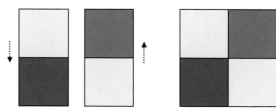

Sew into Four-Patch blocks. Make 162.

If you have a few extra Four-Patch blocks (leftover leftovers!) use them to make a label for the back of the quilt or a small pillow to go with the quilt.

ASSEMBLING THE QUILT TOP

Refer to the Quilt Assembly Diagram.

1. Arrange the Four-Patch blocks. Note the placement of the blocks to create the diagonals. Stand back and look at your arrangement. Balance the eye-catching fabrics.

2. Place the side and corner triangles.

3. Sew the side triangles and Four-Patch blocks together in diagonal rows. Press the seams in alternate directions from row to row.

4. Sew the rows together. Press.

5. Sew the corner triangles to the quilt top. Press the seams toward the corner triangles.

6. Trim 1″ away from the corners of the Four-Patch blocks all around the quilt.

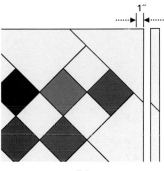

Trim.

7. Layer the top with the batting and backing. Quilt and bind as desired (see page 86).

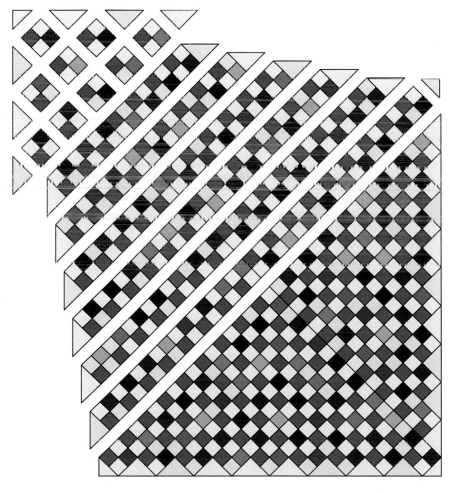

Quilt Assembly Diagram

Mud Pie

INGREDIENTS

- 1 jar (12.25 ounces) caramel ice cream topping

- 2 bars (1.55 ounces each) milk or dark chocolate candy, broken into small pieces

- 1 cup pecan halves, toasted*

- 1 container (½ gallon) vanilla ice cream

- 1 container (½ gallon) chocolate ice cream

- Vegetable oil spray

To toast pecans, preheat oven to 350°. Spread pecans in a single layer on a cookie sheet. Bake 10–12 minutes or until lightly toasted and fragrant; cool completely.

Crust

- 12 pecan shortbread cookies

- 3 tablespoons butter or margarine

1. Combine caramel ice cream topping and chocolate pieces. Microwave on high 1–1½ minutes, stirring every 30 seconds until melted and smooth. Cool slightly.

2. Lightly spray pie plate with vegetable oil spray. Place cookies in resealable plastic food storage bag; crush into fine crumbs. You should have 1¼ cups of crumbs. Place butter in microwave on high, 30–45 seconds or until melted. Stir in cookie crumbs. Firmly press crumb mixture onto bottom of pie plate. Place in freezer.

3. Reserve ½ cup of the toasted pecan halves for the top. Coarsely chop remaining pecans. Set aside.

4. Scoop half of the slightly softened vanilla ice cream over crust, pressing into an even layer. Drizzle with ⅓ of the caramel-chocolate sauce and half the chopped pecans. Place in freezer until ice cream layer is firm.

5. Scoop half of the slightly softened chocolate ice cream over the first layer. Drizzle with half of the remaining sauce and sprinkle with the remaining chopped pecans. Place in freezer until ice cream layer is firm.

6. Scoop the remaining vanilla ice cream around the edge of the pie. Scoop the remaining chocolate ice cream in the center. Top with reserved pecan halves and drizzle with remaining sauce. You will have a heaped and mounded mud pie. (Who wants a skinny mud pie?) Wrap loosely with aluminum foil; place in freezer. Freeze until firm, at least 4 hours.

7. Before serving, refrigerate dessert 30 minutes for easier slicing. Cut into wedges. To make cutting easier, dip your knife into warm water and wipe it dry after cutting each wedge. This dessert can be made and frozen several days in advance of serving.

Apple Crisp Quilt

his quilt focuses on working with all neutrals, including both quilter's neutrals and true neutrals. Choose cool true neutrals such as black, white, and shades of gray or warm quilter's neutrals such as muslin and tan (with darker tans edging toward or including browns). In my quilt, I included all three values—lights, mediums, and darks. Most of my neutrals are the warmer tans, beiges, and muslins. These are the lights. I included brown to create higher contrast because browns are medium and dark. I have also included a few of the true neutrals. The warm muslins and tans remind me of the baked apples and crisp topping, while the browns spice things up, similar to cinnamon, nutmeg, and brown sugar.

FINISHED QUILT SIZE
88½″ × 96½″

note:

This is a scrappy quilt. If you plan to work from your stash, refer to Cutting (below) for the specific sizes of each fabric. If you plan to buy fabric, refer to Yardage for what you need to purchase.

YARDAGE

- ¼ yard each of 45 different fabrics for blocks, or you can duplicate fabrics for a less scrappy look

- Border fabric: 3¼ yard

- Backing fabric: 8 yards (horizontal seam)

- Binding fabric: ¾ yard

- Batting: 94″ × 102″

CUTTING

Assorted fabrics

- From each of 24 different fabrics, cut 1 strip 5″ × 42″; from these cut 8 squares 5″ × 5″ for a total of 192 squares for Half-Square triangles.

- From the remaining 21 fabrics, cut 2 strips 2½″ × 42″ for a total of 42 strips for Four-Patch blocks.

Border fabric
✳ *It's a good idea to measure your quilt before cutting borders (see page 85).*

- Cut 2 strips lengthwise 8½″ × 72½″ for the top and bottom borders.

- Cut 2 strips lengthwise 8½″ × 96½″ for the side borders.

Binding fabric

- Cut 10 strips 2″ × 42″.

CONSTRUCTION
Make sure your ¼″ seam allowance is accurate—all blocks assume an accurate ¼″ seam.

HALF-SQUARE TRIANGLES
Use 192 of the 5″ × 5″ squares to make 192 Half-Square triangle blocks. When you choose pairs of fabrics, be sure there is contrast between the chosen pairs. Each pair of squares yields 2 Half-Square triangle blocks.

1. Pair 2 squares right sides together. Draw a diagonal line on the wrong side of the lighter square. Note: This will be the cutting line, not the sewing line.

Draw diagonal line.

2. Draw another set of lines a scant ¼″ from the drawn lines. These are your sewing lines. If you have a ¼″ presser foot, you can omit this step. Sew a scant ¼″ away from the center line on both sides.

Sew scant ¼″ from center line.

3. Cut on the center line.

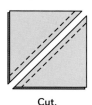

Cut.

4. Press the seam allowances toward the darker fabric.

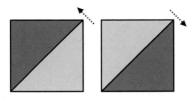

Press. Make 192.

5. Trim each block to 4½″ × 4½″. (See page 13 for trimming instructions.)

FOUR-PATCH BLOCKS

Use 42 of the 2½″-wide strips to make Four-Patch blocks. When you choose strips, be sure there is contrast between the chosen pairs.

1. Pair 2 strips right sides together. Sew the strips together.

Sew strips together.

2. Press the seam toward the darker fabric. Cut the strips into 16 segments, each 2½″ wide.

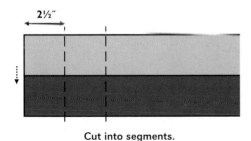

Cut into segments.

3. Arrange 2 matching segments as shown, and sew them together.

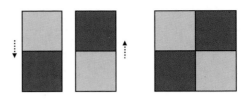

Sew into Four-Patch blocks. Make 168.

ASSEMBLING THE QUILT TOP

Refer to the Quilt Assembly Diagram on page 46.

1. Arrange 192 Half-Square triangle blocks and 168 Four-Patch blocks as shown. Note that 96 of the Four-Patch blocks are in the quilt top and 72 Four-Patch blocks create the inner border.

2. Sew the quilt top together in rows. Press the seams in opposite directions from row to row.

3. Sew the rows together. Press.

4. Sew the top and bottom borders to the quilt top. Press the seams toward the borders. Sew the side borders to the quilt top. Press. (See page 85 for more on adding borders.)

5. Layer the top with the batting and backing. Quilt and bind as desired (see page 86).

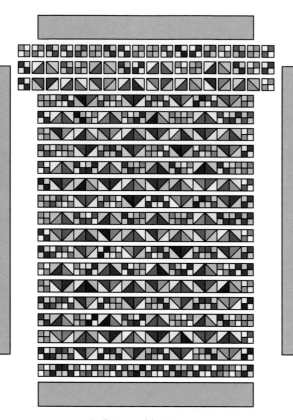

Quilt Assembly Diagram

Neutral Composition,
Cate Franklin,
63½″ × 69½″
(Quilted by Therese Strothman)

SWEET TREATS

Apple Crisp

When fall is in the air, there's nothing like apple crisp to add just the finishing touch to a meal. Plus, you can eat the leftovers for breakfast the next morning.

INGREDIENTS

- 6 medium Granny Smith apples, peeled and *not too thickly sliced* (6 cups total)

- 1½ cups brown sugar, packed

- 1 cup flour

- 1 cup oats

- ½ cup pecans, chopped *(optional)*

- 1½ teaspoons cinnamon

- 1½ teaspoons nutmeg

- ⅔ cup butter, softened

1. Preheat oven to 375°. Grease square pan, 8″ × 8″ × 2″. Place apple slices in pan.

2. In a bowl, mix remaining ingredients thoroughly until mixture is crumbly. Spread over apples.

3. Bake 30 minutes or until apples are tender and topping is golden brown. Serve warm with whipped cream or ice cream.

This is a great recipe for other fruits, too. Try cherries, blueberries, or blackberries. You may need to adjust the amount of sugar.

Serves 6.

Blueberry Cobbler Quilt

*I*t's time to focus on color **and** value. *Blueberry Cobbler* is a monochromatic (one color) quilt. The color family is, obviously, blue. Of course, I had to use different values of blue to create contrast. You can use your choice of color as long as you work with light, medium, and/or dark fabrics in the color family you have chosen. And you don't have to use all three values, just one color and at least two different values of that color. Don't worry if the blues (or your chosen color) don't match. I chose bright blues, gray blues, and some aqua blues. Choose blues you like, not necessarily blues that go together. Make sure that the fabric you choose for your background contrasts well with all of your other fabrics.

FINISHED QUILT SIZE

$76\frac{1}{4}$" × $76\frac{1}{4}$"

note:

This is a scrappy quilt. If you plan to work from your stash, refer to Cutting (below) for the specific sizes of each fabric. If you plan to buy fabric, refer to Yardage for what you need to purchase.

YARDAGE

- 6 yards of light blue fabric for background

- 12 different blue fabrics for blocks (see page 52 for color references):*

  - ¼ yard each of fabrics 1, 2, 3, 4

  - ⅜ yard each of fabrics 5, 7, 8

  - ⅓ yard of fabric 6

  - ½ yard each of fabrics 9, 10, 11

  - ⅝ yard of fabric 12

*Fabric #1 will be in the center of the quilt and fabric #12 will be near the outer edges

- Backing fabric: 5 yards

- Binding fabric: ⅝ yard

- Batting: 82" × 82"

CUTTING

Fabric #1

- Cut 1 strip 5" × 42"; from this, cut 2 squares 5" × 5" for Half-Square triangle blocks.

Fabric #2

- Cut 1 strip 2½" × 42" for Four-Patch blocks.

Fabric #3

- Cut 1 strip 5" × 42"; from this, cut 6 squares 5" × 5" for Half-Square triangle blocks.

Fabric #4

- Cut 2 strips 2½" × 42" for Four-Patch blocks.

Fabric #5

- Cut 2 strips 5" × 42"; from these cut 10 squares 5" × 5" for Half-Square triangle blocks.

Fabric #6

- Cut 3 strips 2½" × 42" for Four-Patch blocks.

Fabric #7

- Cut 2 strips 5" × 42"; from these, cut 14 squares 5" × 5" for Half-Square triangle blocks.

Fabric #8

- Cut 4 strips 2½" × 42" for Four-Patch blocks.

Fabric #9

- Cut 3 strips 5" × 42"; from these, cut 18 squares 5" × 5" for Half-Square triangle blocks.

Fabric #10

- Cut 5 strips 2½" × 42" for Four-Patch blocks.

Fabric #11

- Cut 3 strips 5" × 42"; from these, cut 22 squares 5" × 5" for Half-Square triangle blocks.

Fabric #12

- Cut 6 strips 2½" × 42" for Four-Patch blocks.

Background fabric

- Cut 9 strips 5" × 42" for Half-Square triangle blocks; from these cut 72 squares 5" × 5".

- Cut 9 strips 2½" × 42"; from these, cut 144 squares 2½" × 2½" to add to Half-Square triangle block corners.

- Cut 21 strips 2½" × 42" for Four-Patch blocks.

- Cut 3 strips 10" × 42"; from these, cut 11 squares 10" × 10". Cut the squares diagonally twice to make 44 side triangles.

- **Optional:** Cut 2 squares 9" × 9". Cut the squares diagonally once to make 4 corner triangles.

Binding fabric

- Cut 8 strips 2" × 42".

CONSTRUCTION

Make sure your ¼″ seam allowance is accurate—all blocks assume an accurate ¼″ seam.

❋ *The directions specify blue fabrics. If you chose a different color, substitute the color you chose in the directions.*

HALF-SQUARE TRIANGLES

Use 72 of the 5″ × 5″ assorted blue squares and 72 of the 5″ × 5″ background squares to make 144 Half-Square triangle blocks. Each pair of squares yields 2 Half-Square triangle blocks.

1. Pair 1 blue square and 1 background square right sides together. Draw a diagonal line on the wrong side of the background square. Note: This will be the cutting line, not the sewing line.

Draw diagonal line.

2. Draw another set of lines a scant ¼″ from the drawn lines. These are your sewing lines. If you have a ¼″ presser foot, you can omit this step. Sew a scant ¼″ away from the center line on both sides.

Sew scant ¼″ from center line.

3. Cut on the center line.

Cut.

4. Press the seam allowances toward the darker fabric.

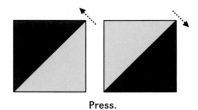

Press.

5. Make 144 Half-Square triangle blocks as follows:

- 4 blocks using the background fabric and fabric #1
- 12 blocks using the background fabric and fabric #3
- 20 blocks using the background fabric and fabric #5
- 28 blocks using the background fabric and fabric #7
- 36 blocks using the background fabric and fabric #9
- 44 blocks using the background fabric and fabric #11

6. Trim each block to 4½″ × 4½″. (See page 13 for trimming instructions.)

HALF-SQUARE TRIANGLE BLOCK CORNERS

1. Draw a diagonal line on the wrong side of all 144 of the 2½″ × 2½″ background squares.

Draw diagonal line.

2. Pair 1 Half-Square triangle block with 1 background square. Place the smaller square on the dark triangle as shown. Sew on the drawn line.

Sew on drawn line.

3. Flip the smaller triangle over so the right side is visible and press the seam toward the darker fabric.

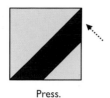

Press.

4. Carefully trim the seam allowance to ¼".

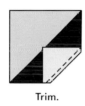

Trim.

5. Repeat Steps 2–4 for all 144 Half-Square triangle blocks.

FOUR-PATCH BLOCKS

Use 21 of the 2½"-wide blue strips and 21 of the background strips to make Four-Patch blocks as follows:

1. Pair 1 background strip with 1 fabric #2 strip, right sides together. Sew the strips together.

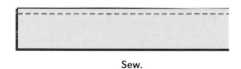

Sew.

2. Press the seam toward the darker fabric. Cut the strips into 16 segments, each 2½" wide.

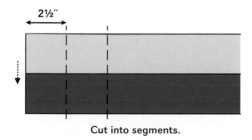

Cut into segments.

3. Arrange 2 segments as shown, and sew them together. Make 8 Four-Patch blocks.

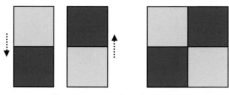

Sew into Four-Patch blocks.

4. Use 2 background strips and 2 fabric #4 strips. Sew them together as in Step 1. Press the seams toward the darker fabric. Cut into 32 segments 2½" wide. Make 16 Four Patch blocks.

5. Use 3 background strips and 3 fabric #6 strips. Sew them together as before. Press the seams toward the darker fabric. Cut into 48 segments 2½" wide. Make 24 Four-Patch blocks.

6. Use 4 background strips and 4 fabric #8 strips. Sew them together. Press the seams toward the darker fabric. Cut into 64 segments 2½" wide. Make 32 Four-Patch blocks.

7. Use 5 background strips and 5 fabric #10 strips. Sew them together. Press the seams toward the darker fabric. Cut into 80 segments 2½" wide. Make 40 Four-Patch blocks.

8. Use 6 background strips and 6 fabric #12 strips. Sew them together. Press the seams toward the darker fabric. Cut into 96 segments 2½" wide. Make 48 Four-Patch blocks.

ASSEMBLING THE QUILT TOP

Refer to the Quilt Assembly Diagram on page 52.

1. Arrange the Half-Square triangle blocks, Four-Patch blocks, and side triangles.

2. Sew the blocks and side triangles together in diagonal rows. Press the seams in opposite directions from row to row.

3. Add the corner triangles last if you are using them. Press the seams toward the corner triangles.

4. Trim the edges 2¾″ from the points of the dark patches in the blocks.

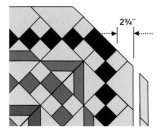

Trim edges.

5. Layer the top with the batting and backing. Quilt and bind as desired (see page 86).

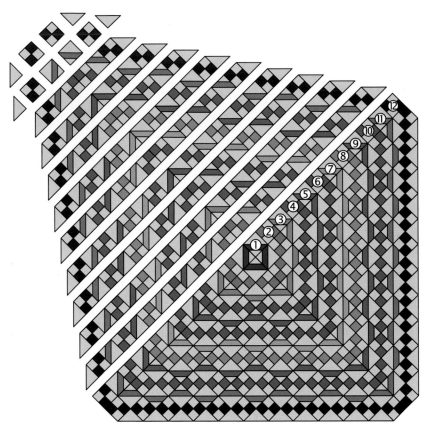

Quilt Assembly Diagram

Blueberries and Cream,
Joseph Pepia,
81½″ × 80″
(Quilted by David Rincon)

SWEET TREATS

Peach Cobbler for Mike,
Cate Franklin,
88¼″ × 89″
(Quilted by Kathy Staley)

Blueberry Cobbler with a Cherry on Top,
Suzanne Barsness,
74½″ × 74½″
(Quilted by Becky Kraus)

Blueberry Cobbler

This recipe is inspired by 15-year-old Nate Kudlich. His mom says this recipe would be famous if Nate didn't eat every bit of this cobbler each time he made it. You'll feel that way, too, when you taste it! The only change I made to Nate's original recipe was to use 3 cups of blueberries (he used 2 cups).

INGREDIENTS

- ⅔ cup flour

- ½ cup sugar

- 1½ teaspoons baking powder

- ¼ teaspoon salt

- ⅔ cup milk

- 2 tablespoons butter

- 3 cups blueberries, fresh or frozen, cleaned and washed or drained

Note: If you are using frozen blueberries, use the small wild ones, and make sure there is no excess ice on them—this makes the cobbler watery and somewhat messy, although still yummy.

1. Preheat the oven to 350°.

2. In a medium bowl, combine the flour, sugar, baking powder, and salt. Stir in the milk, and mix the batter until it is smooth. It will be thin.

3. Melt the butter and pour it into a 9″ × 9″ baking dish. You can preheat the baking dish and melt the butter in it as the oven is preheating. Be careful that the butter doesn't get brown. Pour in the batter and sprinkle the blueberries evenly on top.

4. Bake the cobbler for 40–45 minutes or until it is lightly browned on top and firm in the middle. Serve, adding whipped cream or ice cream if desired.

Makes 9 servings.

Pumpkin Pie Quilt

This quilt focuses on color and value. It is another monochromatic quilt, and this time the color is orange. Did I really say that? Yes. My value of orange is dark orange, also known as rust. Rust is a color seldom chosen by quilters because it is a member of that awkward orange family, but when you use rust in a quilt, it looks very rich, very much like autumn, and very elegant. It says warmth and richness in a way few colors can. The cream background is a warm neutral. Also note that there are several browns in this quilt; browns are created from oranges with gray or black added.

FINISHED QUILT SIZE

67″ × 82½″

note:

This is a scrappy quilt. If you plan to work from your stash, refer to Cutting (below) for the specific sizes of each fabric. If you plan to buy fabric, refer to Yardage for what you need to purchase.

YARDAGE

- ¼ yard each of 18 different medium and dark rust fabrics for Four-Patch blocks and sashing

- 1 fat eighth each of 12 different medium and dark rust fabrics for Half-Square triangles

- 2½ yards of cream fabric for Half-Square triangles, side triangles, corner triangles, and squares

- Border fabric: 2⅛ yards

- Backing fabric: 5 yards

- Binding fabric: ⅝ yard

- Batting: 73″ × 88″

CUTTING

Medium and dark rust

- From each of the 18 different medium and dark rusts, cut 2 strips 2″ × 42″ for a total of 36 strips for Four-Patch blocks and sashing.

- From each of the 12 different fat eighths, cut 3 squares 5″ × 5″ for a total of 36 squares for Half-Square triangle blocks.

Cream fabric

- Cut 5 strips 5″ × 42″; from each strip, cut 8 squares 5″ × 5″ until you have a total of 36 squares for Half-Square triangles.

- Cut 2 strips 12½″ × 42″; from these strips, cut 5 squares 12½″ × 12½″. Cut each square diagonally twice for side triangles.

- Cut 1 strip 14″ × 42″; from this strip, cut 2 squares 14″ × 14″. Cut each square diagonally once for corner triangles.

- Cut 1 strip 3½″ × 42″; from this strip, cut 10 squares, 3½″ × 3½″ for setting squares next to side triangles.

Border fabric

✸ *It's a good idea to measure your quilt before cutting borders (see page 85).*

- Cut 2 strips lengthwise 7½″ × 68½″ for side borders.

- Cut 2 strips lengthwise 7½″ × 67″ for top and bottom borders.

Binding fabric

- Cut 8 strips 2″ × 42″.

CONSTRUCTION

Make sure your ¼″ seam allowance is accurate—all blocks assume an accurate ¼″ seam.

HALF-SQUARE TRIANGLES

Use 36 of the 5″ × 5″ medium and rust squares and 36 of the 5″ × 5″ cream squares to make 72 Half-Square triangle blocks. Each pair of squares yields 2 Half-Square triangle blocks.

1. Pair 1 medium or dark rust and 1 cream square right sides together. Draw a diagonal line on the wrong side of the cream square. Note: This will be the cutting line, not the sewing line.

Draw diagonal line.

2. Draw another set of lines a scant ¼" from the drawn line. These are your sewing lines. If you have a ¼" presser foot, you can omit this step. Sew a scant ¼" away from the center line on both sides.

Sew scant ¼" from center line.

3. Cut on the center line.

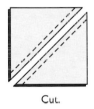

Cut.

4. Press the seam allowances toward the darker fabric.

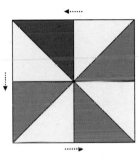

Press. Make 72.

5. Trim each block to 4½" × 4½". (See page 13 for trimming instructions.)

6. Arrange 4 Half-Square triangle blocks randomly to make a Pinwheel block.

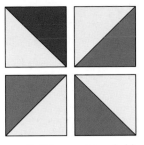

Arrange Half-Square triangle blocks.

7. Sew together and press. Make 18 Pinwheel blocks.

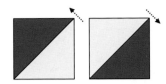

Sew and press. Make 18.

FOUR-PATCH BLOCKS AND SASHING

Use 36 medium and dark rust 2"-wide strips to make the Four-Patch blocks and sashing.

1. Pair 2 strips right sides together. Sew the strips together. Make 18 strip sets.

Sew strips together.

2. Press the seam toward the darker fabric. Cut 16 strip sets into 6 segments 2" wide and 3 segments 8½" wide. Cut 12 segments 2" wide from one remaining strip set, and 14 segments 2" wide from the other. You will have 122 segments 2" wide for the Four-Patch blocks and 48 segments 8½" wide for the sashing.

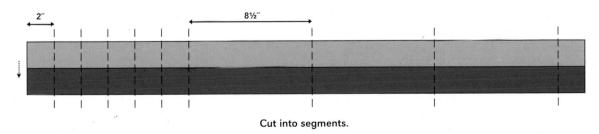

Cut into segments.

3. Arrange matching pairs of 2"-wide segments as shown, and sew them together to make 61 Four-Patch blocks.

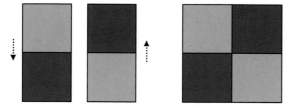

Sew into Four-Patch blocks. Make 61.

ASSEMBLING THE QUILT TOP

Refer to the Quilt Assembly Diagram on page 59.

1. Arrange the Pinwheel blocks, Four-Patch blocks, sashing, and 3½" cream squares as shown. Play with the arrangement until you are satisfied.

Arrange blocks and sashing.

2. Sew 3 Four-Patch blocks and one 3½" cream square together to make a Four-Patch combination block. Press. Make 10 of these blocks.

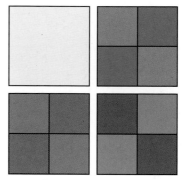

Four-Patch combination block. Make 10.

3. Sew 2 side triangles to each Four-Patch combination block. Press.

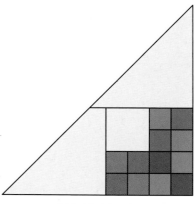

Add side triangles.

4. Sew the single Four-Patch blocks and sashing together in diagonal rows. Press the seams toward the sashing.

5. Sew the Pinwheel blocks and sashing together in diagonal rows. Press the seams toward the sashing.

6. Sew the Four-Patch and sashing rows to the Pinwheel and sashing rows.

7. Sew the assembled side triangle blocks to both ends of the diagonal rows.

8. Sew the rows together. Press.

9. Add the corner triangles last. Press the seams toward the corner triangles.

10. Trim the edges 1″ from the points of the Four-Patch blocks as shown.

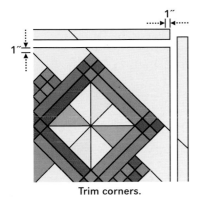

Trim corners.

11. Sew the side borders to the quilt top. Press. Sew the top and bottom borders to the quilt top. Press. (See page 85 for information on adding borders.)

12. Layer the top with the batting and backing. Quilt and bind as desired (see page 86).

Quilt Assembly Diagram

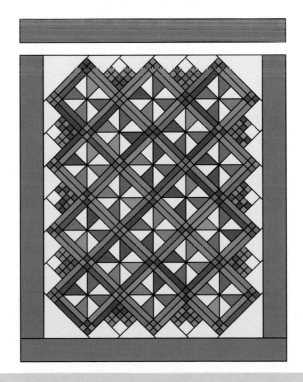

Rhubarb Pie,
Rachel Barsness,
78½″ x 63½″
(Quilted by Becky Kraus)

Periwinkle Pipsqueak,
Joan E. Christ,
35″ x 35″
(Quilted by Therese Strothman)

Pumpkin Chiffon Pie

INGREDIENTS

Filling for 8″ pie

- ½ cup brown sugar (packed)
- 2 teaspoons unflavored gelatin
- ¼ teaspoon each salt, ginger, cinnamon, and nutmeg
- ¾ cup canned pumpkin
- 2 eggs, separated
- ⅓ cup milk
- ¼ teaspoon cream of tartar
- ⅓ cup white sugar

Crust

- 1½ cups fine crumbs (graham crackers or gingersnaps)
- ⅓ cup sugar
- ⅓ cup butter, melted

Whipped cream

- 1 pint heavy whipping cream
- 2 teaspoons real vanilla extract
- 2 tablespoons powdered sugar

1. Preheat oven to 350°.

2. To prepare the crumb crust, mix the crumbs, sugar, and butter together in a bowl. Press and pat the crumb mixture into the pie pan. Bake 8–10 minutes. Set aside to cool.

3. To prepare the chiffon filling, stir together the brown sugar, gelatin, salt, ginger, cinnamon, and nutmeg in a small saucepan. Blend the pumpkin, egg yolks, and milk; stir into brown sugar mixture. Cook over medium heat, stirring constantly, just until mixture boils. Place the pan in a bowl of ice and water or chill it in the refrigerator, stirring occasionally, until the mixture mounds slightly when dropped from a spoon.

4. Beat the egg whites and cream of tartar until foamy. Beat in the white sugar, 1 tablespoon at a time. Continue beating until stiff and glossy. Do not underbeat. Fold the pumpkin mixture into this mixture. Pile into baked pie shell. Chill at least 3 hours or until set.

5. To prepare the whipped cream, whip the cream until soft mounds appear. Add the vanilla extract and powdered sugar. Continue whipping until stiff peaks form. Serve on top of pie slice.

Hot Fudge Sundae Quilt with a Cherry on Top

*I*t is hard to believe that this is a quilt made of neutrals, but it is. Black, white, and shades of gray are true neutrals. Red is added as an accent. This quilt is high in contrast since white is very light and black is very dark. There are also many black-and–white small-scale prints in this quilt. Avoid large-scale prints for the blocks; when cut into smaller pieces, the print may be lost and end up appearing as a solid white or solid black fabric. Feel free to choose a different accent color instead of red—hot pink, lemon yellow, turquoise, or orange are possibilities.

FINISHED QUILT SIZE
78½" × 78½"

YARDAGE

- ¼ yard each of 16 different black-and-white prints that are more white than black for blocks with dark star points

- ¼ yard each of 16 different black-and-white prints that are more black than white for blocks with white star points

- 2 yards solid black fabric (sateen preferred) for blocks

- 2 yards solid white fabric for blocks and sashing posts

- 1½ yards solid red fabric for blocks and sashing

- Border fabric: 3¼ yards if you choose a directional print or 2½ yards of a nondirectional print

- Backing fabric: 7 yards

- Binding fabric: ¾ yard

- Batting: 84" × 84"

❋ *You will be making 9 Star blocks; 5 blocks have black star points, and 4 have white star points. I suggest keeping the two groups of 16 fabrics separate to avoid confusion when making the blocks.*

You will have enough black-and-white prints to make 7 additional blocks, for a quilt of 16 blocks measuring 98½" × 98½". For this larger quilt, you will need an additional 1½ yards of solid black fabric (for a total of 3½ yards), an additional 1½ yards of solid white fabric (for a total of 3½ yards), and an additional 1 yard of red fabric (for a total of 2½ yards). You will also need 3 yards of nondirectional border fabric, 9 yards of backing fabric, ⅞ yard of binding fabric, and batting, 106" × 106".

CUTTING

Black-and-white print fabrics

- From each of the 16 different black and white fabrics in each group, cut 1 strip 2" × 42" and 4 squares, 4" × 4". Keep matching squares and matching strips together.

Solid black fabric

- Cut 4 strips 4" × 42"; from these strips, cut 40 squares 4" × 4" for Half-Square triangle blocks.

- Cut 3 strips 3½" × 42"; from these strips, cut 32 squares 3½" × 3½" for blocks.

- Cut 11 strips 2" × 42" for Four-Patch blocks.

Solid white fabric

- Cut 4 strips 4" × 42"; from these strips, cut 32 squares 4" × 4" for Half-Square triangle blocks.

- Cut 4 strips 3½" × 42"; from these strips, cut 40 squares 3½" × 3½" for Star blocks.

- Cut 9 strips 2" × 42" for Four-Patch blocks.

- Cut 1 strip 2½" × 42"; from this cut 16 squares 2½" × 2½" for sashing posts.

Solid red fabric

- Cut 2 strips 2" × 42" for Four-Patch blocks.

- Cut 12 strips 2½" × 42"; from these strips, cut 24 rectangles 2½" × 18½" for sashing.

Border fabric

❋ *It's a good idea to measure your quilt before cutting borders (see page 85).*

- If your fabric is directional, cut 3 strips 8½" × 42".* Cut 1 strip in half to create 2 rectangles 8½" × 21". Sew one 21" piece to one 42" piece to create a 63" piece. Cut this piece 62½" long for the top and bottom borders.

- Cut 2 strips lengthwise 8½" × 78½" for the side borders.

*If your fabric is not directional, all borders can be cut lengthwise and won't need to be pieced.

Binding fabric

- Cut 9 strips 2" × 42".

Making the Star Blocks

Notice that the blocks with black star points (see the photo on page 62) feature black-and-white prints that are more white than black. The Star blocks with white points feature black-and-white prints that are more black than white. There are 2 Star blocks with black points that repeat the black-and-white prints, but they are in different positions. In the photo, they are in the upper left corner and lower right corner.

Before you begin making your blocks, choose the black-and-white print fabrics that you want in the same block. Choose from the appropriate groups of 16 fabrics. You will need 4 different black-and-white prints in each Star block. I chose fabrics that were dissimilar in pattern design to create eye-catching blocks. For example, in the same block I included a black-and-white check, a black-and-white stripe, and black-and-white polka dots. I prefer this look to a block that includes, for example, only black-and-white print polka dots.

You will then need to decide which 2 black-and-white prints you want in the Four-Patch blocks and which 2 black-and-white prints you want in the Half-Square triangle blocks. Two of the blocks with black star points will use the same fabrics. Simply use them for different parts of the blocks. (See the blocks in the quilt's upper left corner and lower right corner.) You will have extra strips and extra squares. These can be used for another project or for additional blocks if you want a larger quilt.

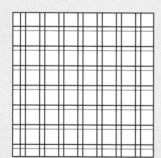 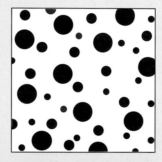

More white than black

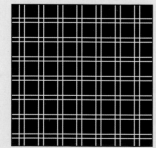 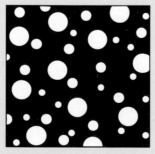

More black than white

CONSTRUCTION

Make sure your ¼″ seam allowance is accurate—all blocks assume an accurate ¼″ seam.

HALF-SQUARE TRIANGLES FOR BLACK STAR POINTS

Use 4 squares 4″ × 4″, 2 each of black-and-white prints (more white than black) and 8 solid black squares to make 16 Half-Square triangle blocks.

1. Pair 1 black and 1 black-and-white print square right sides together. Draw a diagonal line on the wrong side of the lighter square. Note: This will be the cutting line, not the sewing line.

Draw diagonal line.

2. Draw another set of lines a scant ¼″ from the drawn lines. These are your sewing lines. If you have a ¼″ presser foot, you can omit this step. Sew a scant ¼″ away from the center line on both sides.

Sew scant ¼″ from center line.

3. Cut on the center line.

Cut.

4. Press the seam allowances toward the solid black fabric.

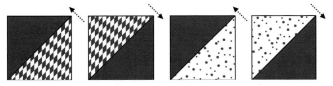

Press. Make 8 of each combination (16 total).

5. Trim each block to 3½″ × 3½″. (See page 13 for trimming instructions.)

6. Repeat Steps 1–5 four times, pairing black-and-white print squares and solid black squares to create 64 additional Half-Square triangles. Keep like prints together.

HALF-SQUARE TRIANGLES FOR WHITE STAR POINTS

Repeat Steps 1–5 above with 4″ squares of 8 black-and-white prints that are more black than white and 4″ solid white squares to create 64 Half-Square triangles. Keep like prints together.

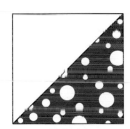

Make 64.

FOUR-PATCH UNITS FOR STAR BLOCKS WITH BLACK POINTS

1. Combine 1 strip of solid black fabric, 2″ × 42″, with 1 strip of a black-and-white print (more white than black), 2″ × 42″. Sew the strips together as shown.

Sew.

2. Press the seams toward the black strip. Cut into 14 sections 2″ wide.

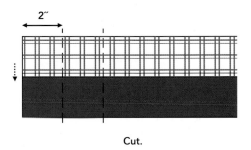

Cut.

3. Make 6 Four-Patch units. Press the seams to one side. Save the 2 additional "half" Four-Patch block units for later. These will be combined with a red/black unit to make 1 of the Four-Patch units in the center of the star.

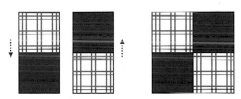

Sew into Four-Patch units.

4. Repeat Steps 1–3 with another strip of solid black fabric, 2″ wide, and 1 strip 2″ wide of a different black-and-white print that is more white than black. Cut this into 8 sections 2″ wide. Make 4 Four-Patch units for the corners of the Star block.

5. Repeat Steps 1–4 four times, pairing print strips and solid black strips to create 24 more Four-Patch units, 8 more "half" Four-Patch blocks, and 16 more Four-Patch units for the corners of the black Star blocks.

FOUR-PATCH UNITS FOR STAR BLOCKS WITH WHITE POINTS

Repeat Steps 1–5 as for the black star points, combining 2″ strips of 8 black-and-white prints (more black than white) with 2″ solid white strips. Keep like prints together. You will need 4 Four-Patch units from each set of strips for the Four-Patches in the corners, and 6 Four-Patch units and 2 "half" Four-Patch units for the other Four-Patch blocks.

Sew into Four-Patch units.

HALF FOUR-PATCH UNITS

1. Sew 1 solid black strip 2″ × 42″ to 1 red strip 2″ × 42″.

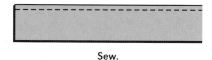

Sew.

2. Press the seam toward the black fabric. Cut the strips into 10 segments, each 2″ wide.

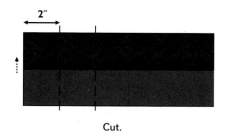

Cut.

3. Combine these units with the half Four-Patch units with solid black fabric to make 10 Four-Patch units.

Sew into Four-Patch units. Make 10.

4. Sew 1 solid white strip, 2″ × 42″, to 1 red strip, 2″ × 42″.

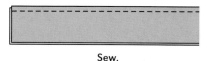

Sew.

5. Press the seam toward the red. Cut into 8 segments 2″ wide.

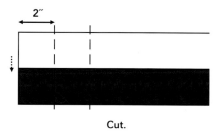

Cut.

6. Combine these units with the half Four-Patch units and solid white fabric to make 8 Four-Patch units.

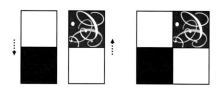

Sew into Four-Patch units. Make 8.

ASSEMBLING THE BLOCKS WITH BLACK STAR POINTS

1. Arrange 16 Half-Square triangles, 10 Four-Patch units, 2 Four-Patch units with a red square, and 8 white 3½″ × 3½″ squares as shown.

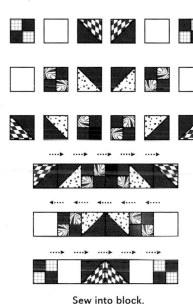

Sew into block.

2. Sew together in rows. Press the seams in opposite directions from row to row. Sew the rows together.

3. Repeat to make 4 more Star blocks with black points, for a total of 5.

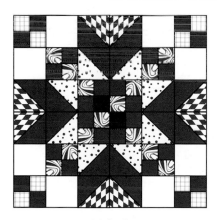

Make 5.

ASSEMBLING THE BLOCKS WITH WHITE STAR POINTS

1. Arrange 16 Half-Square triangles, 10 Four-Patch units, 2 Four-Patch units with a red square, and 8 black 3½″ × 3½″ squares as shown.

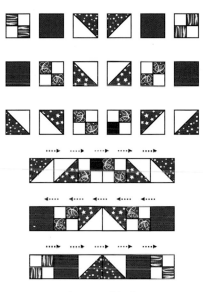

Sew into block.

2. Sew together in rows. Press the seams in opposite directions from row to row. Sew the rows together.

3. Repeat to make 3 more Star blocks with white points, for a total of 4

Make 4.

ASSEMBLING THE QUILT TOP

1. Arrange the Star blocks, sashing strips, and sashing posts as shown, alternating the blocks with black and white star points.

2. Sew together the block and sashing rows. Press the seams toward the sashing.

3. Sew together the sashing and sashing post rows. Press the seams toward the sashing.

4. Sew the rows together. Press the seams toward the sashing rows.

5. Sew the 8½″ × 62½″ border pieces to the top and bottom of the quilt, paying attention to the direction of the print if you are using a directional print. Press the seams toward the border. (See page 85 for more on adding borders.)

6. Sew the 8½″ × 78½″ border pieces to the sides of the quilt top, again paying attention to the direction of the print. Press the seams toward the border.

7. Layer the top with the batting and backing. Quilt and bind as desired (see page 86).

Quilt Assembly Diagram

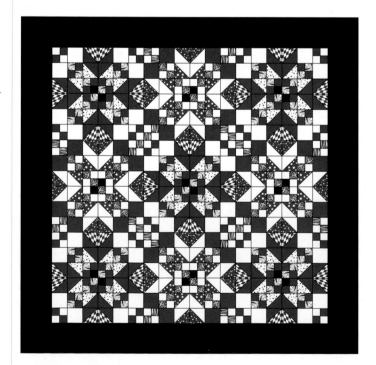

VARIATION
Eliminate sashing and posts.

Strawberry Sundae,
Therese Strothman,
62¾" × 62¾"

Lemon Drops and Licorice,
Mary Louise Washer,
77¼" × 77¼"
(Quilted by Barbara Day)

Homemade Hot Fudge Sauce

This recipe is one of my son Ben's favorites. Whenever he comes home from college, it's one of the first things he wants. It is best served warm the first night, but will keep well in the refrigerator. When you reheat it, reheat only what you need. I take a spoonful or two, put it in a small bowl, and heat it in the microwave for 20–30 seconds. It keeps longer when you don't reheat the entire quantity.

This recipe is very easy—no candy thermometer required! My husband teases me because I prefer more hot fudge sauce than ice cream when I make my sundae!

INGREDIENTS

- ¾ cup unsweetened cocoa
- ¼ cup vegetable oil
- 1 cup milk
- ¼ teaspoon salt
- 2 cups white sugar
- ¼ cup light corn syrup
- 2 tablespoons butter (not margarine)
- ½ teaspoon real vanilla extract

1. Whisk together the cocoa and oil. Add milk.

2. Stir (with a whisk) until smooth.

3. Heat over medium-high heat, stirring constantly. Add salt, sugar, and corn syrup. Boil for 5 minutes. Remove from heat and add butter and vanilla.

4. Serve warm.

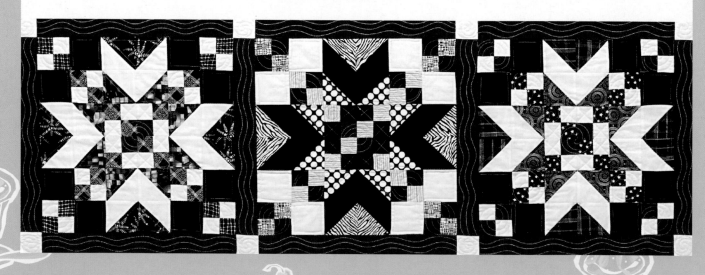

Periwinkle Cupcake Quilt

This quilt focuses on color and value. It is another monochromatic quilt with a neutral background. This time, the neutral is white. And the single color is blue-violet, sometimes called periwinkle. This quilt whispers calmness and serenity. I found that periwinkle is an easy color to like, but often a challenging color to find in a quilt shop. Be careful not to choose fabrics that are actually purple or blue rather than periwinkle. Remember that periwinkle has both blue and violet (purple) in it. I started choosing fabric by looking at both the blues and purples in the fabric store. If there were fabrics with the blues that looked purple, often they were periwinkle. If there were fabrics with the purples that looked blue, often they were periwinkle, too. See if this helps you select true periwinkles.

FINISHED QUILT SIZE

68¾″ × 85½″

note:

This is a scrappy quilt. If you plan to work from your stash, refer to Cutting (below) for the specific sizes of each fabric. If you plan to buy fabric, refer to Yardage for what you need to purchase.

YARDAGE

- ½ yard each of 9 different medium and dark periwinkle fabrics for blocks

- 2¼ yards white fabric for blocks

- 1¼ yards light periwinkle fabric for the side and corner triangles

- ½ yard dark periwinkle fabric for the inner border

- 2¼ yards medium periwinkle fabric for the outer border

- Backing fabric: 5 yards

- Binding fabric: ⅝ yard

- Batting: 75″ × 92″

CUTTING

Medium and dark periwinkle fabrics

- From each of the 9 different fabrics, cut 1 strip 3½″ × 42″.

  From each strip, cut 12 squares 3½″ × 3½″ for a total of 108 squares for Half-Square triangle blocks. (You may get only 11 squares from 1 strip; cut an extra square from the yardage if needed. There is enough fabric.)

- From each of the 9 different fabrics, cut 2 strips 1¾″ × 42″ for a total of 18 strips for small Four-Patch units and strip units.

- From each of the 9 different fabrics, cut 1 strip 3″ × 42″. From this strip, cut 8 squares 3″ × 3″ for blocks.

- From 4 of the darkest medium and dark periwinkle fabrics, cut 1 additional strip 3″ × 42″ for a total of 4 strips for large Four-Patch units. Set them aside. Do not cut them.

White fabric

- Cut 10 strips 3½″ × 42″; from these strips, cut 108 squares 3½″ × 3½″ for Half-Square triangle blocks.

- Cut 18 strips 1¾″ × 42″ for small Four-Patch units and strip units.

- Cut 3 strips 3″ × 42″; from these strips, cut 36 squares 3″ × 3″ for blocks.

Light periwinkle fabric

- Cut 5 squares 13″ × 13″. Cut these diagonally twice to yield 20 side triangles.

- Cut 2 squares 10½″ × 10½″. Cut these squares diagonally once to yield 4 corner triangles.

Dark periwinkle fabric

- Cut 8 strips 2″ × 42″ for inner border.

Medium periwinkle fabric

✺ *It's a good idea to measure your quilt before cutting borders (see page 85).*

- Cut 2 strips 6½″ × 74½″ for the side outer borders and 2 strips 6½″ × 68¾″ for the top and bottom outer borders.

Binding fabric

- Cut 8 strips 2″ × 42″.

CONSTRUCTION

Make sure your ¼″ seam allowance is accurate—all blocks assume an accurate ¼″ seam.

HALF-SQUARE TRIANGLES

Use the 3½″ × 3½″ medium and dark periwinkle squares and the the 3½″ × 3½″ white squares, to make 24 Half-Square triangle blocks for each of the fabrics for a total of 216 Half Square triangle blocks. Each pair of squares yields 2 Half-Square triangle blocks.

1. Pair 1 periwinkle and 1 white square right sides together. Draw a diagonal line on the wrong side of the lighter square. Note: This will be the cutting line, not the sewing line.

Draw diagonal line.

2. Draw another set of lines a scant ¼″ from the drawn lines. These are your sewing lines. If you have a ¼″ presser foot, you can omit this step. Sew a scant ¼″ away from the center line on both sides.

Sew scant ¼″ from center line.

3. Cut on the center line.

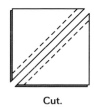

Cut.

4. Press the seam allowances toward the darker fabric.

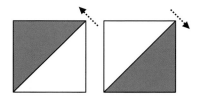

Press. Make 216.

5. Trim each block to 3″ × 3″. (See page 13 for trimming instructions.)

SMALL FOUR-PATCH UNITS

Use 9 different 1¾″-wide periwinkle strips and 9 of the 1¾″-wide white background strips to make Four-Patch blocks.

1. Pair 1 periwinkle strip and 1 white strip right sides together. Sew the strips together.

Sew strips together.

2. Press the seam toward the darker fabric. Cut each strip set into 16 segments, each 1¾″ wide.

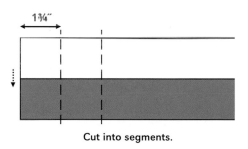

Cut into segments.

3. Arrange 2 segments as shown, and sew them together. Make 72 units.

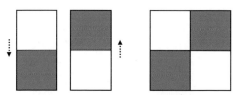

Sew into Four-Patch units. Make 72.

STRIP BLOCKS

Use the remaining 1¾"-wide periwinkle strips and nine 1¾"-wide white strips to make strip blocks.

1. Pair 1 periwinkle strip and 1 white strip right sides together. Sew the strips together.

Sew strips together.

2. Press the seam toward the periwinkle fabric. Cut each strip set into 8 segments, each 3" wide. Make 72 blocks.

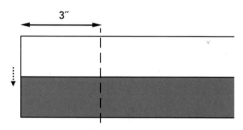

Cut into segments. Make 72.

LARGE FOUR-PATCH BLOCKS

Use 4 of the 3"-wide darkest medium and dark periwinkle strips to make Four-Patch blocks.

1. Pair 1 dark periwinkle strip and 1 medium periwinkle strip right sides together. Sew the strips together.

Sew strips together.

2. Press the seam toward the dark periwinkle fabric. Cut each strip set into 10 segments, each 3" wide.

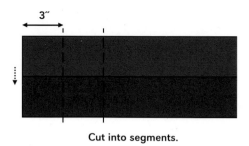

Cut into segments.

3. Arrange 2 segments as shown, and sew them together. Make 10 blocks.

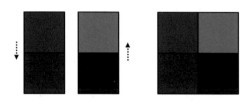

Sew into Four-Patch blocks. Make 10.

ASSEMBLING THE BLOCKS

Note that you will make 6 blocks with a white background and 12 blocks with a periwinkle background. Because of this, you will have extra periwinkle squares.

1. Arrange the Half-Square triangles, small Four-Patch blocks, 3" strip blocks, 3" periwinkle square, and 3" white squares as shown on the next page. The blocks with a white background include 4 white 3" × 3" squares and 1 periwinkle 3" × 3" square.

2. Sew together in rows, pressing the seams in opposite directions from row to row. Sew the rows together to make a Periwinkle Cupcake block. Repeat to make 6 blocks with a white background.

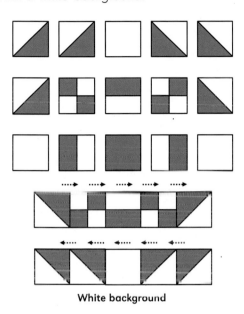

White background

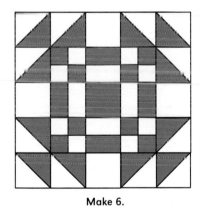

Make 6.

3. Arrange the Half-Square triangles, small Four-Patch blocks, 3″ strip blocks, 3″ periwinkle squares, and 3″ white square as shown. Sew together in rows. Sew the rows together. Make 12 blocks with a periwinkle background.

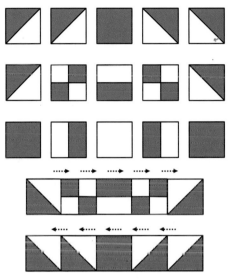

Periwinkle background

Make 12.

ASSEMBLING THE QUILT TOP

Refer to the Quilt Assembly Diagram.

1. Arrange the Periwinkle Cupcake blocks, large Four-Patch blocks, side triangles, and corner triangles. Alternate the blocks with white and periwinkle backgrounds as shown.

2. To make the large side triangle units, sew 1 large Four-Patch block and 1 side triangle together. Press toward the triangle. Trim the triangle so that it is even with the Four-Patch block. Add a second triangle. Make a total of 10 Four-Patch/side triangle combinations.

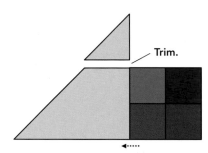

Trim triangle even with Four-Patch.

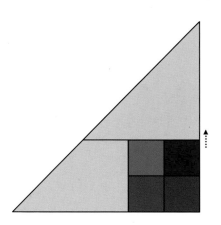

Add second triangle.

3. Sew the side triangle units and blocks together in diagonal rows. Align the seams carefully and pin so that the blocks will meet accurately. Press the seams in opposite directions from row to row. Sew the rows together. Add the corner triangles last. Press the seams toward the triangles.

4. Trim the edges ⅜″ from the points of the Periwinkle Cupcake blocks.

Trim.

5. Sew the 2″ inner border strips together with a diagonal seam. Cut 2 strips 71½″ long for the side inner borders and cut 2 strips 56¾″ long for the top and bottom inner borders. Add the side inner borders to the quilt top, then the top and bottom inner borders. (See page 85 for more on adding borders.)

6. Add the side outer borders to the quilt top, then the top and bottom outer borders.

7. Layer the top with the batting and backing. Quilt and bind as desired (see page 86).

Quilt Assembly Diagram

Chocolate Blueberry,
Rachel Barsness,
63″ × 80″
(Quilted by Becky Kraus)

Periwinkle Cupcakes

INGREDIENTS

- 2 cups white flour
- 1½ cups sugar
- 1 tablespoon baking powder
- 1 teaspoon salt
- 1 cup milk
- ½ cup shortening, such as Crisco*
- 2 teaspoons vanilla extract
- 4 egg whites
- Muffin tins and paper baking cups

*To get a periwinkle color, use a white shortening.

1. Preheat oven to 350°.

2. In a mixing bowl, stir together the flour, sugar, baking powder, and salt. Add milk, shortening, and vanilla to the flour mixture. Beat with an electric mixer on low speed until combined. Beat on medium speed for 2 minutes.

3. Add unbeaten egg whites. Beat on medium speed 2 minutes more, scraping the sides of the bowl frequently.

4. Line muffin pans with paper baking cups. Fill each cup half full. Bake about 20 minutes or until done. Cool 5 minutes in pans. Remove from pans, cool completely, and ice with Creamy Frosting.

Makes 24–28 cupcakes

CREAMY FROSTING INGREDIENTS

- 1¼ cups shortening, such as Crisco*
- 1 teaspoon almond extract
- 5½–6 cups powdered sugar
- ¼–⅓ cup milk
- Purple and blue paste or gel food coloring (not liquid colors). These are available in many kitchen shops and bakery supply stores.
- Optional: sprinkles and blueberries for garnish

1. In a mixing bowl, beat shortening and almond extract with electric mixer on medium speed about 30 seconds.

2. Gradually add about half of the powdered sugar, beating well.

3. Add ¼ cup of the milk.

4. Gradually beat in remaining powdered sugar and enough of the remaining milk to make the frosting a spreading consistency.

5. Add a bit of purple food coloring and mix well, then add blue, a little at a time, until you get periwinkle.

6. Frost cupcakes.

If desired, decorate each cupcake with sprinkles and a single blueberry on top.

Key Lime Pie Quilt

$\mathcal{T}$his quilt focuses on two colors that are opposite on the color wheel—yellow green and red violet. Colors that are opposite on the color wheel are called complementary colors; complementary colors always look good together. I used a variety of fabrics in this quilt. My yellow greens were almost always light and bright, although occasionally they appear more grayed. Therefore, to create contrast, my red violets were medium and dark. I also threw in black here and there to get even more contrast. Black, being a neutral, can be added to any quilt, and it will create wonderful contrast because no color is as dark as black.

FINISHED QUILT SIZE

72½" × 72½"

note:

This is a scrappy quilt. If you plan to work from your stash, refer to Cutting (below) for the specific sizes of each fabric. If you plan to buy fabric, refer to Yardage for what you need to purchase.

YARDAGE

- ⅛ yard each of 36 different light- and medium-value yellow-green fabrics for triangle blocks

- ¼ yard each of 36 different medium- and dark-value red-violet and black fabrics for blocks

- 2½ yards of black fabric for Four-Patch blocks

- Backing fabric: 5 yards

- Binding fabric: ⅝ yard

- Batting: 78" × 78"

CUTTING

Yellow-green fabrics

- From each of the 36 fabrics, cut 1 strip 3" × 42".

From each strip, cut 2 squares 2½" × 2½" for a total of 72 squares, then cut 7 squares 3" × 3" for a total of 252 squares for Half-Square triangle blocks.

Red-violet and black fabrics

- From each of the 36 fabrics, cut 1 strip 3" × 42".

From each strip, cut 2 squares 2½" × 2½" for a total of 72 squares, then cut 7 squares 3" × 3" for a total of 252 squares for Half-Square triangle blocks.

- From 22 of the red-violet fabrics (choose the medium-value ones, not light, bright, or eye-catching/high contrast ones), cut 1 strip 3½" × 42" for a total of 22 strips for Four-Patch blocks.

Black fabric

- Cut 22 strips 3½" × 42" for Four-Patch blocks.

Binding fabric

- Cut 8 strips 2" × 42".

CONSTRUCTION

Make sure your ¼" seam allowance is accurate—all blocks assume an accurate ¼" seam.

HALF-SQUARE TRIANGLES

Use the 252 yellow-green 3" × 3" squares and the 252 red violet, and black 3" × 3" squares to make 504 Half-Square triangle blocks. Pair 7 matching yellow-green squares with 7 matching red violet or black squares to make 14 identical Half-Square triangles. Repeat with the other red violet or black and yellow-green fabrics. Keep like fabrics together. Each pair of squares yields 2 Half-Square triangle blocks.

1. Pair the squares right sides together. Draw a diagonal line on the wrong side of the lighter square. Note: This will be the cutting line, not the sewing line.

Draw diagonal line.

2. Draw another set of lines a scant ¼" from the drawn lines. These are your sewing lines. If you have a ¼" presser foot, you can omit this step. Sew a scant ¼" away from the center line on both sides.

Sew scant ¼" from center line.

3. Cut on the center line.

Cut.

4. Press the seam allowances toward the darker fabric.

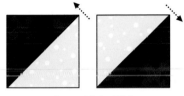

Press. Make 504.

5. Trim each block to 2½˝ × 2½˝. (See page 13 for trimming instructions.)

ASSEMBLING THE TRIANGLE BLOCKS

1. Work with like fabrics and arrange 1 red violet or black 2½˝ × 2½˝ square, 7 Half-Square triangles, and 1 yellow green 2½˝ × 2½˝ square.

Arrange the blocks.

2. Sew together in rows. Press the seams in opposite directions from row to row.

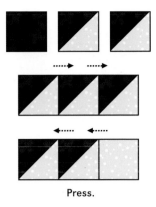

Press.

3. Sew the rows together to create a Triangle block. You will make 2 identical Triangle blocks.

4. Repeat with other red violet or black 2½˝ squares, Half-Square triangles, and yellow green squares to make 72 Triangle blocks.

FOUR-PATCH BLOCKS

Use 22 of the medium red violet 3½˝ strips and 22 of the black 3½˝ strips to make Four-Patch blocks.

1. Pair 1 red violet strip and 1 black strip right sides together. Sew the strips together.

Sew strips together.

2. Press the seam toward the darker fabric. Cut the strips into 8 segments, each 3½˝ wide.

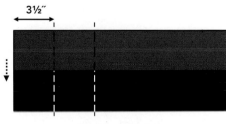

3½˝

Cut into segments.

3. Arrange 2 segments as shown, and sew them together. Make 88 blocks. You will use 72 and have 16 extra.

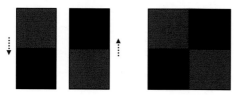

Sew into Four-Patch blocks. Make 88.

ASSEMBLING THE QUILT TOP

Refer to the Quilt Assembly Diagram.

1. Arrange 72 Triangle blocks and 72 Four-Patch blocks. Step back and look at your arrangement. Balance the eye-catching fabrics. Arrange the Four-Patch blocks that are alike in diagonal rows if desired.

2. Sew the blocks together in rows. Press the seams in opposite directions from row to row. Sew the rows together.

3. Layer the top with the batting and backing. Quilt and bind as desired (see page 86).

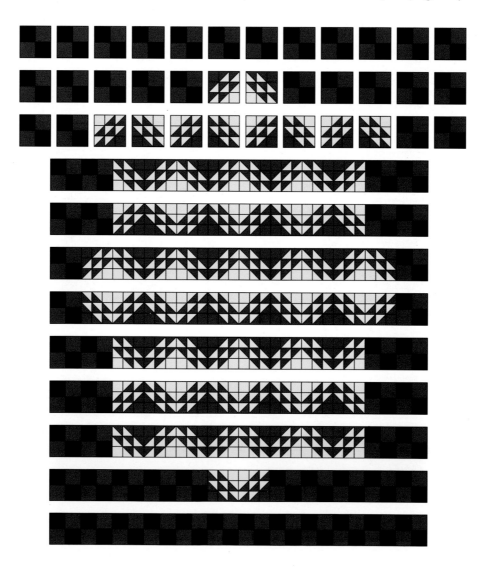

Quilt Assembly Diagram

Plummy Key Lime Pie with a Golden Crust,
Ann Elizabeth Rindge,
71½″ × 71½″
(Hand quilted by Becky Kraus)

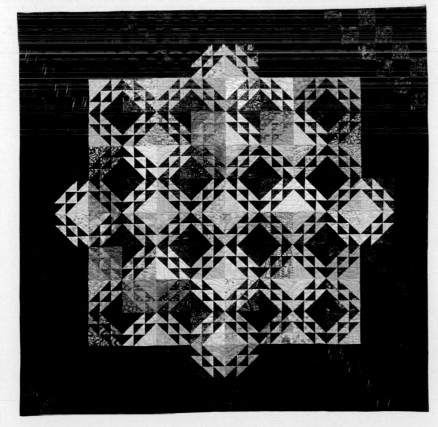

Untitled,
Merry Maricich,
69¾″ x 68½″
(Quilted by Patsi Hanseth)

Key Lime Pie

INGREDIENTS

- 2 cans, 14 oz. each, sweetened condensed milk
- ¾ cup key lime juice
- 2 large eggs
- 1 pint heavy whipping cream
- 4 tablespoons powdered sugar
- 2 teaspoons real vanilla extract

Crust

- 1¼ cups graham cracker crumbs
- 2 tablespoons white sugar
- 4 tablespoons butter, softened

1. Preheat oven to 325°.

2. Mix graham cracker crumbs, white sugar, and butter with a fork, then with your hands. Press firmly into a 9″ or 10″ pie plate. Bake for 15 minutes or until lightly browned. Remove and let stand until cool.

3. Whisk together condensed milk, lime juice, and eggs until well blended. Pour into crust. Bake for 20–30 minutes (or longer) until set. Chill 4 hours.

4. Whip heavy cream until soft peaks form. Add powdered sugar and vanilla extract. Continue whipping until stiff peaks form. Spread over pie, or, if desired, spoon over individual serving slices.

Quilting Basics

Fabric requirements are based on a 42″ width; many fabrics shrink when washed, and widths vary by manufacturer. In cutting instructions, strips are generally cut on the crosswise grain.

SEAM ALLOWANCES

A ¼″ seam allowance is used for all projects. It's a good idea to do a test seam before you begin sewing to check that your ¼″ is accurate.

PRESSING

In general, press seams toward the darker fabric. Press lightly in an up-and-down motion. Avoid using a very hot iron or over-ironing, which can distort shapes and blocks.

BORDERS

I usually cut borders on the lengthwise grain to avoid seams. However, if a fabric is directional or if you don't have enough fabric to cut the borders on the lengthwise grain, it is sometimes necessary to cut them crossgrain. When border strips are to be cut on the crosswise grain, diagonally piece the strips together to achieve the needed lengths.

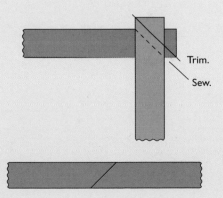
Trim.
Sew.

Butted Borders

In most cases the side borders are sewn on first. When you have finished the quilt top, measure it through the center vertically. This will be the length to cut the side borders. Place pins at the centers of all four sides of the quilt top, as well as in the center of each side border strip. Pin the side borders to the quilt top first, matching the center pins. Using a ¼″ seam allowance, sew the borders to the quilt top and press.

Measure horizontally across the center of the quilt top including the side borders. This will be the length to cut the top and bottom borders. Repeat pinning, sewing, and pressing.

BACKING

Make the backing at least 2″ larger than the quilt top on all sides.

To economize, you can piece the back with a horizontal seam or piece together leftover fabrics or blocks in your collection.

BATTING

The type of batting to use is a personal decision; consult your local quilt shop. Cut batting approximately 2″ to 3″ larger on all sides than your quilt top.

LAYERING

Spread out the backing wrong side up and tape the edges down with masking tape. (If you are working on carpet you can use T-pins to secure the backing to the carpet.) Center the batting on top, smoothing out any folds. Place the quilt top right side up on top of the batting and backing, making sure it's centered.

BASTING

If you plan to machine quilt, pin baste the quilt layers together with safety pins placed a minimum of 3″–4″ apart. Begin basting in the center and move toward the edges, first in vertical, then horizontal, rows.

If you plan to hand quilt, baste the layers together with thread using a long needle and light-colored thread. Knot one end of the thread. Using stitches approximately the length of the needle, begin in the center and move out toward the edges.

QUILTING

Quilting, whether by hand or machine, enhances the pieced design of the quilt. You may choose to quilt in-the-ditch, echo the pieced motifs, use patterns from quilting design books and stencils, or do your own free-motion quilting.

BINDING

These directions are written for a double-fold straight-grain binding (French Fold)

Trim excess batting and backing from the quilt. If you want a ¼″ finished binding, cut the strips 2″ wide and piece them together with a diagonal seam to make a continuous binding strip.

Press the seams open, then press the entire strip in half lengthwise with wrong sides together. With raw edges even, pin the binding to the edge of the quilt a few inches

away from the corner, and leave the first few inches of the binding unattached. Start sewing, using a ¼″ seam allowance.

Stop ¼″ away from the first corner (see Step 1); backstitch 1 stitch. Lift the presser foot and needle. Rotate the quilt a quarter turn. Fold the binding at a right angle so it extends straight above the quilt (see Step 2). Then bring the binding strip down even with the edge of the quilt (see Step 3). Begin sewing at the folded edge.

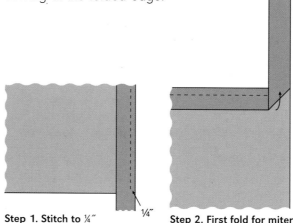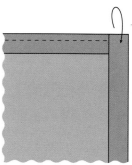

Step 1. Stitch to ¼″ from corner. ¼″

Step 2. First fold for miter

Step 3. Second fold alignment. Repeat in the same manner at all corners.

Finishing the Binding

Method 1:

Fold under the beginning end of the binding strip ¼″. Lay the ending binding strip over the beginning folded end. Continue stitching the seam beyond the folded edge. Trim the excess binding. Fold the binding over the raw edges to the quilt back and hand stitch, mitering the corners.

Method 2:

Fold the ending tail of the binding back on itself where it meets the beginning binding tail. From the fold, measure and mark the cut width of your binding strip minus ⅛″. Cut the ending binding tail to this measurement. For example, if your binding is cut 2¼″ wide, measure from the fold on the ending tail of the binding 2⅛″ and cut the binding tail to this length.

Open both tails. Place 1 tail on top of the other tail at right angles, right sides together. Mark a diagonal line and stitch on the line. Trim the seam to ¼″. Press open.

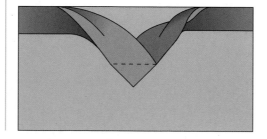

About the Author

Sandy Bonsib is a teacher by profession and a quilter by passion. She has a graduate degree in education and has taught and lectured locally since 1993 and nationally since 1997. This is her eighth book (her first for C&T Publishing). She has appeared on *Lap Quilting* with Georgia Bonesteel, *Simply Quilts* with Alex Anderson, and was one of six featured artists on "Quilts of the Northwest," 1998. In 2003 she was nominated for teacher of the year. Sandy also coordinates Quilts for the Children, a group that has made almost 5,000 quilts for the children of battered women. She mentors high school students doing their senior projects in quiltmaking. She also is a professional quilt appraiser.

Sandy lives on a small farm on Cougar Mountain in Issaquah, Washington, with her family and many animals. She also raises puppies for Guide Dogs for the Blind.

For information about Sandy's classes and lectures, visit her website at www.sandybonsib.com.

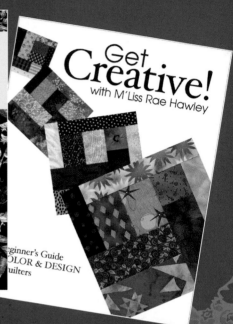

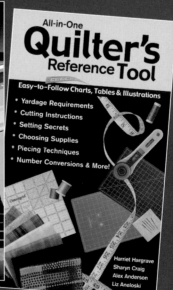